Flowers
of Silk & Gold

Flowers of Silk & Gold

FOUR CENTURIES OF OTTOMAN EMBROIDERY

SUMRU BELGER KRODY

MERRELL

in association with

THE TEXTILE MUSEUM, WASHINGTON, D.C.

First published on the occasion of the exhibition *Flowers of Silk and Gold: Four Centuries of Ottoman Embroidery* at The Textile Museum, Washington, D.C., February 18–July 30, 2000

Published 2000 by Merrell Publishers Limited
www.merrellpublishers.com
© 2000
The Textile Museum
2320 S Street, NW
Washington, D.C. 20008-4088
www.textilemuseum.org

Distributed in the USA & Canada by Rizzoli International Publications, Inc. through St Martin's Press, 175 Fifth Avenue, New York, New York 10010

British Library Cataloguing-in-Publication Data
Krody, Sumru Belger
Flowers of silk and gold : four centuries of Ottoman embroidery
1.Embroidery, Ottoman 2.Gold embroidery 3.Decoration and ornament – plant forms
I.Title II.Textile Museum
746.4'4'0956

ISBN 1 85894 105 9 (hardback only)

Produced by Merrell Publishers Limited
42 Southwark Street, London SE1 1UN

Edited by Iain Ross

Printed and bound in Italy

Front jacket/cover: Cover fragment, 17th or early 18th century. Detail from The Textile Museum 1.22. (cat. no. 9)

Frontispiece: Bohça (wrapping cloth), late 19th century. Detail from The Textile Museum 1962.46.1 (cat. no. 22)

Photo Credits

© The Textile Museum, photographed by Franko Khoury
Cat. nos. 1–3, 5, 7–10, 12–57
© The Textile Museum, photography courtesy of Sotheby's, New York; photographed by David Hays
Cat. nos. 4, 6, 11
© Eric Krody
Figs. 1–4
© Sumru Belger Krody
Figs. 5, 6, 23–29
© Österreichische Nationalbibliothek, Vienna
Fig. 30
© Deutsches Archäologisches Institut, İstanbul
Fig. 31
© Topkapı Palace Library, İstanbul
Figs. 32, 33, 40, 41
© Victoria and Albert Museum Picture Library, London
Fig. 34
© Demirbank, İstanbul
Fig. 35
© Deniz Müzesi Kitaplığı, İstanbul
Fig. 36
© Sevgi Gönül Collection, İstanbul
Fig. 37
© The Royal Library, National Library of Sweden, Stockholm
Fig. 38
© Rijksmuseum, Amsterdam
Fig. 39

Contents

Foreword

This volume, celebrating The Textile Museum's seventy-fifth anniversary, introduces the rich variety of Ottoman embroidered textiles held by the museum.

The Textile Museum's holdings of close to one hundred embroidered textiles in the Ottoman tradition are significant in their quantity and quality. Rarely viewed or published until now, these textiles offer themselves as a resource for our knowledge of Ottoman culture.

The textiles selected for exhibition may be divided into two categories: home furnishings and articles of clothing. Each was created to define a space or facilitate a social act or ritual. These objects link the private to the public world. As author Sumru Belger Krody suggests in her exploration of the domestic environment in which these textiles were made and used, these are objects that tacitly represent the social contract – that tie the people who made them and used them to one another, and to the external world.

George Hewitt Myers, founder of The Textile Museum, began his collection of Ottoman embroideries in 1915 with two round floor spreads (cat. nos. 1 and 2). In the 1920s and 1930s, Mr. Myers focused on collecting large covers, wrapping cloths (*bohça*s), turban covers, and floor spreads of the seventeenth and eighteenth centuries. His eye for quality was unwavering.

In more recent years, other donors have enriched The Textile Museum's collections of Turkish embroideries. I have known or known of several of these donors and am aware that these textiles, precious to the owner, have been lovingly donated in order that they may have a permanent home in which they and their companion pieces form a meaningful corpus. Mr. and Mrs. William O. Baxter, who presented the rare barber's set, and Leila F. Wilson, who contributed several napkins (*yağlık*s) and headscarves (*çevre*s), collected these objects as a result of their foreign service experiences. David Dew Bruner is a judicious collector who has consistently sought to collect fine pieces of embroidery. He has donated eighteen choice examples to The Textile Museum collection. A gift of a prayer cloth by Mrs. Jale Çolakoğlu came into the collection itself attentively wrapped in a contemporary *bohça*.

The embroideries in the museum's collection evoke words such as 'ceremony,' 'belief,' and 'beauty,' words understood by those who made them and those who collected them. My thanks to all the donors who have followed George Hewitt Myers's footsteps in building this outstanding collection.

Those individuals and organizations acknowledged in this volume, who have helped to make this exhibition and publication possible, are fostering an understanding and appreciation of Ottoman culture. We greatly appreciate their generosity and support.

Ursula Eland McCracken
Director
The Textile Museum

Acknowledgments

The Textile Museum wishes to acknowledge with gratitude the generous financial support of the following individuals and institutions: the American Research Institute in Turkey, Philadelphia; Hannelore and R. Jeremy Grantham, Boston; the Institute of Turkish Studies, Washington, D.C.; the Marshall and Marilyn R. Wolf Foundation, New York; Sotheby's, New York; and Drs. Babette and Marc Weksler, New York.

This book and The Textile Museum exhibition that it accompanies would not have been possible without the support of many individuals and institutions.

The following curators in museums in Turkey and in the United States generously shared their collections and knowledge with me: Selma Delibaş, Dr. Filiz Çagman, Dr. Hülya Tezcan at the Topkapı Sarayı Müzesi, Hülya Bilgi, Şebnem Akalın and Lale Görünür at the Sadberk Hanım Museum, Emel Özkan and Bengi Çorum at the Bursa Türk Islam Eserleri Müzesi, Madelyn Shaw at The Rhode Island School of Design Museum, and Christa Thurman at The Art Institute of Chicago. I am also grateful to Göksenin İleri, Zafer Esi, Mustafa and Füsun Ünlü in Turkey, and David Dew Bruner and Drs. Babette and Marc Weksler in the United States, who were very generous in allowing me access to their collections and in providing information. I also wish to thank the librarians at the Library of Congress and Mary Mallia at The Textile Museum's Arthur D. Jenkins Library.

A grant from the American Research Institute in Turkey in Philadelphia supported my research in Turkey. The Institute of Turkish Studies in Washington, D.C. enabled the purchase of research materials for The Textile Museum's Arthur D. Jenkins Library. The photography, ably coordinated by Anne Weigant, was provided in part by Mary Jo Otsea of Sotheby's, New York, and her excellent and cheerful photography staff; the rest was supported by the Lloyd Cotsen Textile Documentation project.

I would also like to extend my thanks to the Board of Trustees of The Textile Museum and to the museum's staff for their encouragement and congeniality. I am especially indebted to Claudia Brinttenham. The Lloyd Cotsen Textile Documentation Project, and Lloyd Cotsen's steadfast interest in The Textile Museum, refined the technical vocabulary and classification that I relied upon for this publication.

I also owe countless debts to two individuals in particular. First to Carol Bier, Curator of Eastern Hemisphere Collections at The Textile Museum, who provided much-needed advice and support throughout the project, and read and edited the text many times. Secondly to Eric Krody, who supported and encouraged me from the start of the project, and stuck by me throughout this undertaking.

Sumru Belger Krody
Assistant Curator
The Textile Museum

Preface

Embroidery was a traditional decorative art in the Ottoman Empire. Its most sophisticated examples were made in the palaces by master artisans and their apprentices. In the countryside, the skill was passed on from mother to daughter. Embroidery was part of Turkish life, enjoyed at every level of society from the wealthiest to the humblest. It brought color and beauty to people's lives.

It would not be wrong to say that the last generation to practice the art of embroidery was that of my grandmother. By contrast, the generation of my mother, emancipated by Atatürk's reforms, had little time to spare for embroidery. They pursued careers as teachers, doctors, and lawyers. While the recognition of the rights of women was a landmark in Turkey's political, economic, and social progress, it also caused a large drop in the number of women practicing this art. Younger generations acquired new tastes and preferences.

During the last decade or two there has been a revival of interest in this elaborate art form. People have started to rediscover the beauty of embroideries that had hitherto been kept in chests in their attics. They have gradually brought all the splendor of their colors out into the daylight again. I can personally testify to this: after many years I began to display, in a silver bowl in my home, the silk handkerchiefs embroidered by my paternal grandmother. I greatly treasure the silver-embroidered bridal bath towels and the coin purse that once belonged to my maternal grandmother. Today many Turkish families display such valuable samples of embroidery in elegant frames on the walls of their homes. Some families have been generous enough to establish museums to share the embroideries and garments collected by previous generations. These collections contain some wonderful examples of Turkish embroidery, and are still being expanded by their founders and curators.

I feel extremely pleased and honored that The Textile Museum has produced this book and accompanying exhibition on the seventy-fifth anniversary of its foundation. What makes this event even more special is that it coincides with the seven-hundredth anniversary of the founding of the Ottoman Empire, and this constitutes a tribute to Ottoman culture.

Nur İlkin
Wife of His Excellency Baki İlkin,
Ambassador, Republic of Turkey

Introduction

Embroidered textiles offer a unique window onto urban society in the Ottoman Empire. This book, accompanying an exhibition of the same title, is a study of those textiles customarily used in domestic life. It chronicles the history of the urban embroidery tradition in the Ottoman Empire from the early seventeenth century to the early twentieth century with The Textile Museum collection as its focus. Its primary goals are to present these textiles within their historical and cultural context, to explore the history of the embroidery tradition through the changing social and economic aspects of Ottoman culture, and to provide technical information on the embroidery process and structure of these textiles.

The history of this urban embroidery tradition parallels that of the Ottoman Empire, with its changing geography, economy, and social life. From the mid-eighteenth century onwards, the increasing use of naturalistic floral motifs and landscapes, more subdued colors in place of bold ones, and experimentation with shading and perspective indicate the arrival of a new style of decoration from Europe, and point to closer ties, especially artistic and cultural, between the Ottoman Empire and European countries.

During the nineteenth century, affected by changes in the Ottoman and world economies, Ottoman society witnessed the rise of an educated middle class with ever-expanding wealth. This new class was capable of purchasing luxury goods that in previous centuries could have been acquired only by the Palace or by the wealthiest individuals in the empire. Costly silk satin weave and velvet ground fabrics embroidered with metallic threads, sequins, gems, and pearls became fashionable items bought by this emerging middle class.

Embroidery was one of the art forms practiced both commercially and domestically by a large portion of the population of the empire. Both men and women embroidered textiles for sale. Gender was the determining factor in where people worked, at least until the late nineteenth century. Men generally worked in workshops, embroidering heavier materials that would become tents, boots, saddles, quivers, and cuirasses. Both professional and amateur female embroiderers worked at home in more quiet and peaceful parts of the cities, producing smaller articles for use in the home. The study of embroidery, one of the least recognized resources for Ottoman studies, gives a valuable insight into the Ottoman economy and particularly into the significant economic contribution of women through textile production. The role of women in textile production was considered to be subordinate to that of men. Women's duties included those aspects of the process that allowed them to finish their domestic tasks before they turned their attention to textile production. For an urban woman in the empire, embroidery was generally the most common means of contributing to her household's income. Although there have never been official statistics, embroiderers were probably the largest group of female textile workers in the empire.

Ottoman embroidery is unique. It is instantly recognizable, and distinguishable from other embroideries around the world by its style. As in other Ottoman art forms, floral motifs predominate. Although a variety of flowers and trees are depicted in these textiles, a few distinct motifs such as tulips, hyacinths, carnations, bouquets of roses, vases filled with many colorful flowers, as well as weeping willow and cypress trees, are all considered 'typical' Ottoman motifs. Ottoman embroidery was usually executed by counting the warp and weft yarns of a balanced plain-weave ground fabric. This embroidery technique fostered very uniform stitching and minimized irregularities. The fineness of the embroidery depended on the fineness of the ground weave. The finer the ground fabric, the smaller the stitches that could be embroidered. Although the stitch repertory was limited to a few stitches such as running, double running, satin, and Turkish, Ottoman embroiderers were exceptional in their ability to create a great range of different effects by manipulating a single stitch in numerous ways, as well as by their masterly use of metallic threads to enhance their motifs.

Embroidered textiles were an integral part of Ottoman daily life and special occasions such as weddings and other rites of passage. These textiles served many functions, from home furnishings to fashion accouterments. In Ottoman homes, everything was covered and stored or presented wrapped with layers of lavishly embroidered textiles. Rooms were decorated with embroidered hangings, covers, and cushions. Food was served on trays covered with embroidered napkins. Guests dried their hands on embroidered textiles after washing and before gathering around embroidered floor spreads to take a meal. Gifts were given in embroidered bundles. Women's costumes included many embroidered items, such as sashes, headscarves, slippers, robes, and sometimes entire dresses. At weddings, circumcisions, and other ceremonies, embroidered textiles decorated rooms, and were displayed in processions. They were items used to exhibit the wealth of a woman's family and her skill as an embroiderer.

Ottoman urban embroidery tradition can tell us many things about Ottoman social and economic history. As we begin to examine products drawn from this tradition, we will learn more about the makers, methods of production, uses, and users. Thus, this book aims to broaden the spectrum of information available for the study of this subject by introducing the little-known but highly important Textile Museum collection, which is among the foremost in the world in its quantity and quality.

Sumru Belger Krody
Assistant Curator
The Textile Museum

N

Vienna
Pest
Buda
Belgrade   Bucharest   Feodosiya
R. Danube   BLACK SEA
Sofia   Edirne   Trabzon
İstanbul   Amasya
Gelibolu   R. Kızılırmak   Erzurum
Salonika   Ankara
Athens   Bursa   Mosul   R. Tigris
İzmir   Baghdad
Konya   R. Euphrates
Algiers   Aleppo
                                                    Basra
Tunis   Damascus
                          Jerusalem
Tripoli   Alexandria
              Cairo
                                                Medina

ADRIATIC SEA   CASPIAN SEA

R. Don
R. Dnieper

R. Nile   RED SEA   Mecca

                                                San'a

0   500   1000 miles
0   750   1500 km

- - - - The Ottoman Empire at the
        end of the seventeenth century

A Brief History of the Ottoman Empire

The horse dies, the field remains
The hero dies, his legacy remains[1]

Osman and his people formed a small principality of the large Selçuk Sultanate near the region of Bithynia in northwestern Anatolia. They initiated their bid for independence around the turn of the fourteenth century.[2] The capture of Bursa from the Byzantine Empire in 1326 by Osman's son Orhan brought a change to the character of their nomadic border principality.[3] It became a real state with boundaries, a settled population, and a capital. During Orhan's reign, Turkish forces, encouraged by a fight over the Byzantine throne, instead of raiding, began to establish permanent bases in Byzantine territory. They crossed the Dardanelles to Thrace for the first time during this period, establishing a permanent base in Gallipoli (Gelibolu).[4] Expansion into Europe continued with vigor under the command of Murat I, son of Orhan. Adrianople fell to Ottoman forces in 1361 and became Edirne, the second capital of the Ottoman Empire. Thrace and Bulgaria were quickly added to the territories, a strong blow to the Balkan dynasties who were seeking to unite to keep approaches to their Byzantine Empire open. Murat I died on the battlefield at the battle of Kossovo-Polje in 1389. After further victories in the Balkans, Murat I's son Beyazit I turned his attention to the creation of a centralized state by incorporating Turkish dynasties in Anatolia into his empire. Beyazit I's move, and the pleas of the Turkish dynasties, brought Timur, the self-proclaimed heir to the Mongol Empire, to Anatolia. This episode in Ottoman history ended with Beyazit I's crushing defeat at the battle of Ankara in 1402.[5]

After this devastating defeat, the Ottoman Empire spiraled into a decade of civil strife. This ended with the victory of Mehmed I, who took measures to restore stability. Mehmed I's grandson, Mehmed II, was one of the most famous and admired of Ottoman sultans. In the spring of 1453, Mehmed, known as *Fatih* (the Conqueror), commanded the Ottoman forces in their conquest of Constantinople, the most glorious city on earth in the fifteenth century and capital of the Byzantine Empire.[6] Mehmed's announcement that Constantinople, now called İstanbul, would be the new capital of his empire signaled his ambition for universal rule.[7] The borders established during his reign would endure until the nineteenth century as the heartland of the Ottoman Empire.

---

1 Turkish proverb: *at ölür, meydan kalır, yiğit ölür, şan kalır.*
2 Shaw 1977, vol. 1, pp. 12–15
3 *Ibid.*, pp. 17–22
4 İnalcik and Quartaert 1996, pp. 11–12
5 *Ibid.*, p. 12
6 Shaw 1977, vol. 1, pp. 55–62
7 *Ibid.*, pp. 55–70

The grandson of Mehmed the Conqueror, Selim I, continued the expansionist policies of the Ottoman state. During this time, the empire felt strong enough to challenge its eastern and southern neighbors, especially the Mamluks in Egypt. The Ottomans quickly established themselves in Syria and Egypt, occupying the Holy Islamic cities of Mecca and Medina and becoming their protectors in 1571.[8] After these acquisitions, Ottoman sultans started emphasizing their role as 'caliph of all the Muslims in the world.' The greatest of all Ottoman sultans, Süleyman, ascended to the Ottoman throne in 1520 and reigned for the next forty-six years, becoming the longest-ruling sultan.

By the beginning of the seventeenth century, the Ottoman Empire included North Africa, the Middle East, the Balkans, and Eastern Europe, and during the second half of the century the empire reached its greatest territorial extension. The Ottomans engaged European armies and navies in a series of important battles and played a major role in the balance of powers in Europe. But this century was also marked by internal crises. Long wars with the Hapsburgs in the West and with the Safavids in the East brought significant changes to Ottoman political and social life, and exhausted the treasury and the manpower of the empire. Military rebellions were followed by student rebellions, and then rebellions of provincial governors, erupting at intervals throughout the century. The central government's control over Anatolia shifted to the military, to the mercenaries, and to the provincial governors during the rebellions. These rebellions, increasing concessions to internal powers, and the military defeats abroad started to decide the fate of the Ottoman rulers. Mehmed IV's deposition, following the unsuccessful second siege of Vienna in 1683, was one of these events.[9]

Politically and administratively, the eighteenth century looked more peaceful for the Ottoman Empire than previous centuries. Although several wars were fought with the Russians and the Safavids, their outcomes favored the Ottomans, who had increasing help from European countries. New ways of pursuing scientific research and techniques of governing swept through Europe in the eighteenth century, preparing the way for the industrial age. The Ottomans, however, were slower to observe and to react to these changes than the Europeans. The disintegration of the empire's extremely centralized state power, creating an environment that prevented its own smooth functioning, further hindered change. The power of *ayan*s (provincial landowners) increased throughout a long line of incapable sultans and grand viziers in the seventeenth and eighteenth centuries. This power shift, accompanied by the impoverishment of the military and the bureaucracy, contributed to an overall economic decline and lack of interest in education and

---

8 İnalcik and Quartaert 1996, p. 20
9 *Ibid.*, pp. 413–31

the natural sciences among the general populace.[10] Selim III (1789–1807) was the one of the first sultans who realized the need for change. Although he attempted a number of reforms, especially in the army, change was not realized until the beginning of the nineteenth century, during the reign of Mahmud II (1808–39). Mahmud II was a much stronger and more determined reformer than Selim III. After establishing necessary alliances in the first part of his reign, the second was marked by a number of reforms. His first move was once more to centralize the state by reducing the power of *ayan*s in the provinces. His next move was to put an end to the Janissary corps. This, the first standing army in Europe, was established in the fourteenth century as a strong central military force and was instrumental in expanding the Ottoman state. But over the centuries the Janissary corps became a strong political force, so strong that by aligning themselves with other forces in the empire they were able to dethrone several sultans. Janissaries were forbidden to marry or to pursue any career outside of the army. In the mid-sixteenth century, these prohibitions were lifted. Thereafter, members of the Janissary came to share interests with other forces within Ottoman society and lived much as others in society. Thus they took their authority from the populace with which they became closely associated.[11]

The period in Ottoman history between 1839 and 1876 came to be known as Auspicious Reordering, *Tanzimat-ı Hayriye*, corresponding with the reigns of Abdülmecit I and Abdülaziz. This period introduced new legislation and reforms that modernized the Ottoman state and society. Rather than preserving and restoring old government institutions, *Tanzimat* replaced old institutions with altogether new ones. These new institutions guaranteed the lives and property of Ottoman subjects, established a regular system of taxation, and developed equitable systems of conscripting, training, and maintaining soldiers. The only issue that did not please the ruling class was the shift of power from the sultan and Palace to the representative assembly.[12] The first Ottoman constitution, which established a parliamentary government, was proclaimed in 1876. Although dissolved for a short period during the reign of Abdülhamid II (1876–1909), the parliament was restored again in 1908.

The end of World War I in 1918 brought an end to the Ottoman Empire. Having sided with Germany, the Ottoman Empire shared its defeat. Although occupied by the victorious forces in 1918, İstanbul continued to be the seat of the sultan and the capital of the occupied Ottoman Empire. The Ottoman Empire officially ceased to exist with the establishment of the Republic of Turkey in 1923 following a long struggle by the Turkish people under the leadership of Mustafa Kemal, who

---

10 İnalcik and Quartaert 1996, pp. 639–45
11 Shaw 1977, vol. 2, pp. 21–28
12 *Ibid.*, pp. 55–171

came to be called Atatürk. The title of 'caliph of all the Muslims in the world,' held by the Ottoman sultans since 1571, was abolished by the new Republic in 1924, bringing the Ottoman house and the caliphate to an end.

Figure 1
Interior view,
Topkapı Palace harem

During the thirteenth and fourteenth centuries, Anatolia was ethnically and religiously diverse. Large Turkish groups had been pouring into the Anatolian peninsula from the east since the second half of the eleventh century. There were constant conflicts throughout the thirteenth century, most erupting between settled townsmen clustered around large cities, the seats of Selçuk government, and nomadic peoples occupying frontier regions. Townsmen, with their learned society and orthodox Sunni Islamic beliefs, opposed the militant nomads with their heterodox Islamic beliefs, some of which could be traced back to pre-Islamic religious traditions. Osman's people were one of these militant groups and kept that character long after they had settled and mixed with the previously settled population of the region.[13] Very early on, they established policies and rules that were to influence the character of the later Ottoman state they formed, such as the policy of conquest and expansion, and the military structure of governmental institutions. The later success of the house of Osman was also the result of their centralizing policy and their success in preventing fragmentation of their realm.

Ottoman conquests in the Balkans were a threat to Europe that would last for the next four centuries. The Ottomans' move was a signal for the West of future military defeats and the new ethnic mixture in the Balkans. Mass immigration and settlement of Turkish groups from Anatolia to new frontier territories acquired in the Balkans, to guard the borders and raid the land beyond, altered the ethnic composition of the area forever. This immigration followed the pattern of Turkish expansion into Anatolia from the eleventh to the thirteenth century.[14] The Christian population of the Balkans remained, under Ottoman rule. The Ottomans followed their traditional policy of tolerance towards Christians, Jews, and others, who accepted the same God and were 'people of the book.' If they accepted Muslim rule and paid a head tax instead of performing military service, their lives, properties, and freedom of worship were guaranteed. They were also permitted to retain their own legal traditions. Most of the settled population in the Balkans was in favor of Ottoman rule, enjoying lower taxes and a more stable and centralized government, capable of protecting their interests. Christians, Jews, and newly arrived Muslims from the east lived side by side and developed long-lasting interconnected traditions in arts and crafts.[15] Perhaps the best example of this cross-fertilization occurred in İstanbul, the capital of the empire. At the time of its capture in 1453, the city of

13 *Enc. Isl.* 1993, vol. 8, pp. 190–91
14 Shaw 1977, vol. 1, p. 19; İnalcik and
    Quartaert 1996, pp. 14–15
15 Shaw 1977, vol. 1, pp. 27–28

Constantinople had been in decline for so long that Sultan Mehmed's initial effort was to repopulate the city by bringing in Turkish, Jewish, Armenian, and Greek populations from various parts of the empire. His goal was to make İstanbul the religious and economic center of the world. As the protector of Islam, he established himself in İstanbul, invited the Greek Patriarch to remain there and relocated the Armenian Patriarch to take up residence in the city. To establish İstanbul as an economically viable city, he granted commercial privileges to the Italian maritime states and built markets and exchanges to facilitate trade.[16] All these efforts were rewarded, and within two generations, İstanbul became one of the largest and richest cities in the world, with a multilingual, multi-ethnic, and religiously diverse population.

Under Ottoman rule, the population was divided into two main groups: *askeri* (military men and administrators) and *reaya* (the flock: merchants, artisans, peasants). The *reaya*, because they pursued productive activities, paid taxes; the *askeri*, because they performed public services in the name of the sultan, did not. To be part of the *askeri* class an individual had to be born to it. This system was not as rigid as it may now appear and allowed a certain degree of mobility between groups. One way of entering the *askeri* class was to be pressed into service and sent to the Palace school. Those sent included Christians, who were obtained through warfare or the *devşirme*, a regulated human levy imposed on rural Christian populations. These young boys were converted to Islam and taught Turkish. Then the most gifted ones were sent to the Palace to be educated in military and administrative matters, as well as in the arts of civilization, which included Persian and Arabic languages, religious philosophy, and literature. The ones who reached the highest levels in the administration became generals, governors, and viziers (ministers of state). The *reaya* could also enter the *askeri* and rise to the highest levels through education in the *medreses,* which dispensed religious and legal teaching.[17]

Tensions between the forces supporting centralization and decentralization of the Ottoman state profoundly affected social and political life. Power in the state shifted from the capital to the provinces and back again with a corresponding shift in wealth. Centralization of the state during the fifteenth century created a new class clustered around the courts of the sultans and the crown princes. The members of this thriving new class, owing to their education and culture, became 'Ottomans,' making up the élite ruling class. Becoming an Ottoman through education, establishing oneself in the *askeri* class, and settling in İstanbul became a dream of the sons of many Christian and Muslim *reaya*. But although being in the ruling élite was a much sought-after dream, in reality these bureaucrats were slaves of the sultans. Their positions, lives, and wealth depended on the will of the sultan

16 Mansel 1995, pp. 1–16
17 Fleischer 1986, pp. 5–7, 18–25

whom they served. Thus, when a new sultan ascended the throne, he brought his own men with him to replace previous office holders. Ottoman sultans, following the footsteps of earlier Islamic rulers, valued education and learning. They cultivated the arts and surrounded themselves with artists, poets, scholars, and men of science. Well-educated and well-versed scholars were always welcome in their court and favored within the government.

The second half of the sixteenth century brought changes both to the European powers and to the Ottoman Empire. In Europe, the Renaissance was at its height. In the Ottoman state, a shift away from its policy of conquest brought the Ottoman expansion in Europe to a halt, dampening what had been a vigorous frontier spirit, and compromising the guiding principle of the Ottoman Empire.[18] Sultan Süleyman (1520–66) was known to many around the world as the Magnificent, but he was named *Kanuni*, the Law-Giver, by his people, who idolized him for his knowledge and administrative integrity. During his reign, the Ottoman administration was regularized. Islamic law and common law, derived from established usage and from royal decrees, were finally codified and declared the Ottoman Code. These changes increased the administrative needs of the Empire tremendously and caused yet another swell in its bureaucratic hierarchy.

All through these centuries, despite military and political struggles, there was a vigorous trade in artistic and luxury goods between the Ottomans and Europeans. Ottoman silk fabrics were among the most valuable commodities in Europe, used for church vestments and to dress the wealthy élite. European imitation of Ottoman ceramics and metalwork was widespread, as was adaptation of aspects of Ottoman costume and weaponry. As the Ottoman military threat to Europe began to decline after the late seventeenth century, Europe's stereotyped image of the Turkish people began to broaden to include both the wise and compassionate, and the vain and foolish, replacing the deadly fear and admiration of previous centuries. It was about this time that European embassies and travelers began to write of their experiences in Ottoman lands. One of the first and best known of these travelers was Ogier Ghislain de Busbecq, Imperial Ambassador of Ferdinand I of Austria to the court of Sultan Süleyman the Magnificent at Constantinople between 1554 and 1562.

The Age of Enlightenment began in Europe and spread to Ottoman lands in the seventeenth and eighteenth centuries. Around the world, the ideals of reason and the rights of the individual brought profound technological and social changes. New social and political trends were emerging that would shape the colonial world of the nineteenth century. What established the power of each country was now

---

18 İnalcik and Quartaert 1996, pp. 24–25

not so much military victory as accomplishments in science and industry. World markets grew. Finding new markets and maintaining them became an important political concern for countries that wanted to sell their manufactured goods and receive the raw materials to produce more. During the eighteenth century, the Ottoman Empire made greater efforts to establish friendly relations with such European countries as France, Britain, Holland, Sweden, Denmark, and Prussia, which owned the new technologies and were also capable of helping the empire resolve its conflicts with other nations. The first long-term Ottoman embassies were sent to Europe: to Vienna in 1719 and Paris in 1721, followed by permanent embassies to London in 1793, and to Vienna, Berlin, and Paris by 1796. European countries were also in favor of friendly relations with the Ottoman Empire owing to their rising colonial needs. They considered the existence of the Ottoman Empire a strategic necessity, since it was perfectly placed to keep the communication lines open with their ever-expanding distant colonies.[19]

Before the eighteenth century, the empire's internal trade was greater than its external trade. Agriculture supplied the bulk of the revenues. Externally traded goods included a limited variety of finished products, such as textiles. With the expansion of world trade in the eighteenth century came new institutions of banking and credit, first established by the Dutch and English. All these new trends would take on vast proportions in the nineteenth century. Although the Ottoman Empire may have had one of the best systems of collecting state revenues, its economy was lagging behind rapid changes that were taking place elsewhere in the world.[20] The character of Ottoman exports started to shift from manufactured luxury goods to raw materials. Although there was great expansion in manufacturing in Ottoman lands, production never reached European levels.[21]

İstanbul was still the shining capital of a powerful Ottoman Empire in the eighteenth century. But as might be expected, each shift of state power or change in the economy resulted in a change in social structure. This was more apparent in the capital than anywhere else in the empire. The character of the Ottoman élite changed in the eighteenth century. A new type of bureaucrat started filling the ranks of the higher and lower offices of a government that was expanding hugely with each passing century. These bureaucrats were not from hereditary *askeri* families. Nor had they attended the Palace school as *devşirme*s or religious schools. They were the sons of *reaya* who through more liberal education had established themselves in the government and were handling the empire's domestic and foreign affairs in line with changing ideas on government and diplomacy. They were the products of a new informal recruiting system that started among

19 *Encl. Isl.* 1993, pp. 197–198
20 İnalcik and Quartaert 1996, pp. 639–45
21 Quataert 1994, pp. 87–121

high-level bureaucrats in the seventeenth century. Promising young men from the *reaya* were recruited into the households of the élite, and then launched into their careers in government. What they wanted from this worldly success was not what their forebearers expected. After years of wars and rebellions, this generation wanted to make the most of the material pleasures of life. They sought status not from sponsoring civic monuments such as large mosques, but from smaller civic foundations such as libraries, schools, baths, and fountains, and from private establishments such as *yalı*s (shoreline houses), which offered comfort in a transient and unstable world.

Before the eighteenth century, the official Ottoman court art emphasized the might of the Ottoman state, its army and its subjects, its sultan and his dignitaries as victors. Starting in the eighteenth century there was an interest in also representing festive occasions such as weddings and circumcision ceremonies. In these presentations, utmost attention was given to representing the details of these events, their social aspects, and the expressions and reactions of people from all social strata. The period that signaled the change came to be known as the 'Tulip Period,' and corresponded with the reign of Ahmed III (1718–30). It was appropriate to name this artistically active period after the tulip, which was the most cherished flower of the Ottomans. Ahmed III tried to revive "the brilliance of the art and culture of the sixteenth century": what was thought to be the magnificent height of the Ottoman Empire. His approach was purely aesthetic.

During Ahmed III's reign, Yirmisekiz (Çelebi) Mehmed Efendi was sent to Paris as the Ottoman Ambassador. He and his entourage in 1721 created the wave of 'Turquerie' that swept the fashion world and the social life of the French capital for the next few years. Besides his official political mission, Sultan Ahmed III entrusted Efendi with the mission of learning all that he could about French architecture and culture. At his return he brought back many gifts from the French king, scholarly books and architectural drawings as well as information about French society and relations between women and men.[22] For the first time in Ottoman history, European style and culture were considered worthy of imitation. The élite of eighteenth-century Ottoman society started experimenting with contemporary European models of art and technology. They introduced European furnishings in their homes, planted gardens, and constructed pavilions in what was perceived to be a European style. They filled their gardens enthusiastically with old Ottoman favorites, such as jasmine, irises, roses, lilacs, hyacinths, carnations, and tulips, and then copied them in paint inside their new living spaces. Although this experimentation with European styles did not last

22 Goodwin 1997, p. 175

Figure 2
Interior view,
Dolmabahçe Palace

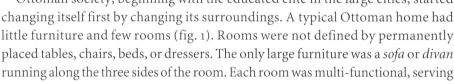

long and did not initially reach large portions of the populace, it formed the basis for later eighteenth- and nineteenth-century art. During this period the seeds of nationalism began to germinate, especially among the non-Muslim populace, who had greater and easier contact with Europeans through trade partnerships. The spirit of nationalism would grow and eventually speed the disintegration of the Ottoman Empire in the nineteenth century.

During the nineteenth century, the Ottoman Empire lost many of its wealthiest, most fertile, and most populated provinces in Europe and Africa, first to nationalist movements, and later to European colonization.[23] This loss was a real economic blow to the Ottoman Empire, which was already in debt from financing wars, especially the Crimean War. Losses in human, mineral, agricultural, and industrial resources aside, the loss of markets for manufactured goods was critical. The bulk of Ottoman trade was internal. Over the last few centuries different parts of the empire had relied heavily on raw materials from other parts of the empire to manufacture and finally sell their goods. Now many industries either suffered shortages of raw materials or could not sell their products. Foreign loans to the Ottoman government and later direct foreign investments in Ottoman industry became the most important factors in the course of the empire's economy until 1918.[24]

Starting in the reign of Mahmud II (1803–39), the Ottomans came to believe that the traditional ways had to be put aside in order to survive and ultimately to reach the level of development that European countries had attained. European culture was no longer a curiosity, as it had been in the eighteenth century, but was rather a thing to be adapted. Gradually change came into the lives of the Ottomans, as they began to wear European clothing, speak European languages, read and discuss European books and ideas, and even enjoy European entertainment. As was generally the case in Ottoman society, the Palace took the lead. Sultan Mahmud dressed like a European monarch, moved to palaces that resembled European ones, and decorated them with European furniture. He was also the first sultan since Süleyman the Magnificent to attend public receptions and entertainments as well as to participate actively in the meetings of his chief officials. Before his reign, sultans were kept away from the populace and were perceived as unapproachable. With the adoption of new European ideals this was changing too.[25]

Ottoman society, beginning with the educated élite in the large cities, started changing itself first by changing its surroundings. A typical Ottoman home had little furniture and few rooms (fig. 1). Rooms were not defined by permanently placed tables, chairs, beds, or dressers. The only large furniture was a *sofa* or *divan* running along the three sides of the room. Each room was multi-functional, serving

23 İnalcik and Quartaert 1996, pp. 761–62
24 *Ibid.*, pp. 766–75
25 Shaw 1977, vol. 2, p. 49

as a place to dine, sleep, or entertain at different times of the day. Glazed tiles or hangings provided decoration on the walls in wealthy homes. From the eighteenth century onwards, decorating the walls with painted friezes depicting landscapes, vases full of flowers, garlands, or flower bouquets became fashionable.[26] By the nineteenth century, chairs, dining tables, and fixed beds appeared in the home (fig. 2). Thus, each room was now designed to serve a specific function such as sleeping, dining, or entertaining. This change required the addition of several rooms to traditional houses and the restructuring of family traditions of eating, sleeping, and interacting with visitors.

In traditional Ottoman society, differences in religion, rank, and class were immediately apparent from the *kavuk*s (turbans) and *kaftan*s (robes) people wore. The acceptance of Western clothing, with its frocks and trousers, obliterated the visual distinctions of rank, class, and religion. Many happily adopted this new style and enjoyed being more readily accepted as equals. In 1829, laws were passed to make 'modern' dress compulsory for all but clerics.[27]

With the *Tanzimat* (see page 15), a centralized government with a new generation of bureaucrats was created. These bureaucrats, appointed by the Palace, spread to the provinces and assumed posts among the 'provincial' people. Besides enforcing the law of the capital, these bureaucrats and their families introduced to the local people new ideas and values from İstanbul. The garments they wore, the furniture they used, the books they read, the ideas they expressed, and even the fact of literacy among the women of these families, became desirable in these provincial towns. The bureaucrats were valuable additions to provincial society and were welcomed eagerly by a large portion of the populace who were already looking towards İstanbul for news, trying to follow the lead set by the court.

The laws established during the *Tanzimat* period, which guaranteed the lives and property of all subjects and the stability of these laws, gave confidence and strength to Ottoman society. The younger generation was raised in a westward-looking world. A new system of secular public schools was established. The army took the lead in developing secular education at the elementary level. Besides the technical schools for engineering and agriculture, museums and libraries were founded for the general public. Learning French or any other European language became preferable to learning Persian or Arabic, which had distinguished the 'educated Ottoman' in preceding centuries.[28] The emergence of a new educated middle class produced an intellectual awakening in society. Simplification of the written Ottoman language by the intelligentsia encouraged more people to read and brought literature to the lower classes.

26 Renda 1978, pp. 711–35
27 Shaw 1977, vol. 2, p. 49
28 *Ibid.*

During this period, Ottomanism was the official policy of the empire, which dictated that all the subjects of the empire were called Ottomans whatever religion they professed. They were equals under the law and held the same rights and duties. But the Ottoman Empire was different from European nations, containing many subjects who differed widely in language, race, and religion. Nationalism, which emerged in the eighteenth century, started taking hold of the many different peoples of the Ottoman Empire. The ideas of 'motherland,' 'liberty,' 'democracy,' and 'constitutionalism' started to appear in Ottoman literature. Since the 1840s, thousand of refugees from Ottoman lands that were lost in wars to other countries or that had declared their independence from the Ottoman Empire had been arriving in Anatolia. This flow became a torrent after the Crimean War (1853–56) with Russia. This influx of peoples with close affinities to the Turkish Muslim population changed the character both of the cities and of the countryside of Ottoman Anatolia. These immigrations, as well as changes taking place in the world economy and the power struggles among European countries at the end of the nineteenth and the beginning of the twentieth century, prepared the Ottoman Empire for a new political structure. After World War I and the war of Turkish independence, the Republic of Turkey was established in 1923 on six principles: republicanism, nationalism, populism, revolutionism, secularism, and statism.[29]

29 Shaw 1977, vol. 2, pp. 373–95

Makers and Methods

With patience
Sour grapes become sweetmeat, and
The leaves of mulberry tree become silk cloth[1]

MAKERS

Foreign visitors to *Kapalı çarşı* (the Grand Bazaar) in İstanbul sometimes looked with awe at the vastness, sometimes with disdain at the narrow streets (fig. 3). Sultan Mehmet the Conqueror built the nucleus, *Bedestan*, in the fifteenth century around which the bazaar grew. Its rents went to the *vakıf* (endowment) of the mosque of Aya Sofya (Hagia Sophia).[2] Every imaginable trade was represented, each one occupying designated streets within this labyrinth. Turkish markets today follow this same pattern. Each street was named according to the trade found there. Merchants who dealt in embroidered articles occupied the *Yağlıkçılar sokak* (street of *yağlık*-makers). *Çıkrıkçılar* was where the shops that sold distaffs and spinning-wheels were located. *Sandal* or *Sendal Bezestan* was for merchants of fine silk fabric. *Dulbend çarşısı* was for plain muslin and turban-dressers. The goods came to *Kapalı çarşı* from across the empire. All were hung in front of the shops, making the streets seem even narrower and more difficult to navigate. Each shop consisted of a platform raised about a half meter from the ground with a small back room or recess. The platform was covered with a carpet or mat, which served both as a seat for the merchant and his customers, and as a counter for the merchant to spread out his goods. This area was flanked by rows of shelves, on which more goods were stacked. *Araba*s (carriages) with lattice windows brought wealthy İstanbul ladies to *Kapalı çarşı*. With the help of a shop apprentice, they shopped through the lattice windows for everything, including embroidered textiles destined to decorate their homes and trousseaus. Although those less privileged walked to the market, the same goods were available so long as they had the money to purchase them. Not only finished products, but also materials for further production or embellishment were sold. Some middle-class ladies preferred to buy the ground fabric, embroidery threads, sequins, and other materials separately to take home and on which to put their creativity to work.

Embroidery was carried out on a number of levels in the Ottoman world, its production varying both in skill and volume. These textiles had many sources of origin; some came from the royal workshops attached to Topkapı Palace[3] or from

Opposite:
Cover fragment, 18th century. Detail from The Textile Museum 1.40 (cat. no. 13)

---

1 Turkish proverb: *sabır ile koruk helva olur, dut yaprakları atlas olur.*
2 Mansel 1995, pp. 128–30
3 *Cemaat-i Zerdüzan* (master embroiderers) worked exclusively for the court. They were six or seven artisans working in a workshop located in the First Court of Topkapı Palace. These artisans were first mentioned at the beginning of the sixteenth century in documents listing salaried artists at the Ottoman court (Delibaş 1987, p. 47).

Figure 3
Kapalı çarşı *today*

the royal workshops in the large urban centers of the empire. Others came from the imperial *harem* or from the *harem*s of other distinguished personages of the empire. Some were products of the private workshops in the old capitals Bursa and Edirne, in the new capital İstanbul, and in other city centers of the empire.[4]

The gender of the embroiderer, at least until the late nineteenth century, was an important element in determining who worked where. However, although men worked in workshops and women at home, both worked on textiles that were destined to be sold. Muslim and Christian women from villages around İstanbul and along the Bosphorus were feeding an ever-hungry İstanbul market. In the late nineteenth century many known workshops were employing young embroiderers of both sexes. One firm in İstanbul, Sadulla-Robert Levy, is said to have employed six hundred male and female embroiderers. The establishment of the Teacher Training School for Girls in İstanbul, and later in other cities, might have brought the number of embroiderers in the workforce to its highest level ever at the turn of this century.[5]

Our earliest record of workshops tells us there were sixty shops in İstanbul in 1628 staffed by one hundred male embroiderers.[6] Those in workshops mainly worked with expensive materials such as pearls, gold, and precious or semi-precious stones on large pieces of heavy material thought to require a man's strength to push the needle through. Canvas, woolen fabric, and leather tents, door curtains, saddle covers, as well as garments and *bohça*s (wrapping cloths) embroidered with heavy gold metallic threads were the major products of these workshops. Records indicate that in some cases embroiderers needed to be supplied with the materials due to their expense. The person who commissioned the piece most often provided the very fine silk ground fabric, precious yarns, metallic threads, pearls, and semi-precious stones.[7] Although few sources describe working conditions in the workshops, there seems to have been a division of labor. Certain workshops specialized in embroidering specific objects, such as the tent or door-curtain makers who clustered in the areas of the bazaar that carried their name. This division of labor was also reflected in the shops that sold the finished products, as seen in many street names of the *Kapalı çarşı*.

Before an embroiderer started work on a piece, professional draftsmen drew designs on the ground fabrics. The source for most designs was the Palace design atelier or *nakkaşhane*. Designs created by *nakkaş*s (design artists) in the royal workshop were transferred to a variety of media by the palace artisans and then disseminated to the public through the professional draftsmen in the bazaars.

4 Such as Aydın, Antep, Bandırma, Draman, Edremit, İskece [Xanthi], Karaman, Milas, Rhodes, Salonica, Crete, Yannina, Beroea, Bursa, Damascus, and Caffa [Feodosiya on the Crimea] (Erber 1995, p. 25).

5 Delibaş 1987, p. 54

6 Johnston 1985, p. 9

7 Gervers 1982, p. 37, footnote 42

Designs on different textiles were very often similar to each other (cat. nos. 50–53). Several draftsmen working in a workshop shared the same design templates or blocks. Professional draftsmen in different workshops probably also used similar templates or blocks. Thus products of different workshops shared the same designs. Buyers, with their preference for certain fashionable designs, also undeniably encouraged the different workshops to produce similar designs.

Domestic embroidery made either for sale or for personal use accounted for a large percentage of all production. Women worked in the *haremlik*s (women's quarters) of their homes in the more peaceful, residential side of the city, away from the hubbub of the city's commercial center. Wooden houses with projecting upper stories lined the narrow cobbled streets. Their adjoining gardens were overhung with mulberry, acacia, and oriental plane and cypress trees, and abundantly adorned with flowers (fig. 4). As women in urban centers were confined by social customs to their houses, embroidery was an appropriate way for them to pass the time. It was a major part of the upbringing of young girls, many of whom would become as skilled as their professional counterparts and would be able to earn money as well as to furnish their own homes. Professional women embroiderers were often engaged in a cottage industry or putting-out system, dependent on orders from shop owners in the bazaars or agents for the provision of raw materials and for retailing or sales. They worked at home with their own tools. Some produced items independently, however. They made uncommissioned items on their own at home, evidently on a quite small scale, and marketed them through intermediaries. Those less well-to-do went into the markets themselves to sell their work.[8] This type of activity can still be seen in Turkey. Most of the time the merchant-financier or agent controlled the quality of the materials, and the fineness and type of stitches used. A famous undated document in the Topkapı Palace archives is especially revealing. It discusses the identity and control of the commissioner and the gender and power of the embroiderers.[9] The document was a report filed with the sultan by an appointee of Topkapı Palace, complaining that many women embroiderers approached with work commissioned by the Palace did not accept it. The work was too difficult, they said. This type of very fine work took a painstakingly long time and the materials cost too much money. The Palace was very specific in what it wanted, up to the number of warp and weft counts for the stitching. The commission called for 1544 grams of silk thread to be used to embroider pieces approximately 250 cm wide and 400 cm long. This commission exemplifies how even the

8 Gerber 1980, p. 237

9 Celâl 1939, p. 29. The letter reads as follows: *İşletmek için emrolunan Çadirşebler cümle yedidir. Her biri beş endir. Otuz beş en olur. On nefer nakış işleyici mutemede hatun bulunmak müyesser olmadi. Bazı ekabire hatunlara birkaç para verdim. Banna hassaten işler gönderdiler deyu bazı yerlerde söylemişler, işidecek ihtiyar etmeyip aldım. Gayri kimesnelere verdim. Ve bazı hatunlar dahi işlemeğe almışlar iken ince iştir, işlemeğe kudretimiz yoktur deyu getirip bıraktılar. İşleyenler dahi günde bir dirhemden ziyade işliyemezler, her bir Çadirşebe dört yüz elli dirhem ve beş yüz dirhem ibrişim*

Palace relied on outside producers to help cover their needs. This document also reveals that the embroiderers were women working independently, with the power to reject requests if they found the work beyond their capacity or the demand unreasonable. This scenario likely recurred many times not only at the Palace level, but with the urban élite as well. In the nineteenth century it was a well-established custom for a well-to-do widow who was known as a good homemaker and skilled embroiderer to set up an informal finishing school for young girls in her neighborhood. These young girls would spend half their time gaining experience in running a household, and the other half learning how to embroider. Their work could either become part of their trousseau or be sold by the widow through an intermediary.[10]

gider. Bunlarin tamam olmasına sol ki makduru bendei aciz ve hakiridir sarfol-unmuştur. Baki ferman devletlu sultanım hazretlerinindir.

10 Kayaoğlu 1998, pp. 12–19

Cover, 18th century.
Detail from The Textile
Museum 1.5 (cat. no. 14)

Figure 5
Spinning and embroi-
dering around the tan-
dor. *Engraving from*
Tableau general de
l'Empire othoman *by*
Ignatius Mouradgea
d'Ohsson (1740–1807),
Imprimerie de monsieur
(Firmin Didot) Paris,
1788–1824

At home, much time was devoted to embroidery. Women were first to get up; after sending their husbands to work and finishing their daily chores, they would sit down with their embroidery. Sometimes women of more than one *harem* gathered together to work and socialize at the same time. Younger women would have occupied themselves with headscarves, towels, sheets, and quilts, or *sofa* and pillow covers for their trousseau or to bedeck their nuptial chambers, while those already wedded would work on pieces for their newborns' rooms and their sons' circumcision beds. Through historical miniatures and drawings, we know that women not only embroidered but were also engaged in spinning yarn in their homes. They might also have woven the ground fabric themselves. Miniatures depicting domestic scenes generally show two types of women's work going on at the same time. One or more women work in front of their embroidery frames, while others spin what appears to be flax, given the large standing distaff they use (fig. 5).[11] The silk threads used by these women were bought from the bazaar. The presence of silk spinners and twisters from the Bursa area in the seventeenth century is a clear indication that silk spinning and twisting were being done from early on in workshops by professionals.[12]

The skill of Ottoman embroiderers was recognized and admired worldwide. Women embroiderers called *bulya*s were in high demand, especially in Eastern

11 Baines 1989, pp. 25–59
12 Gerber 1988, pp. 63–65

European aristocratic houses of the sixteenth and seventeenth centuries.[13] Several letters have survived written by Hungarian noblewomen asking to borrow a *bulya* from a sister, or asking for an exchange of patterns with Turkish women living in Hungary at the time. An Italian traveler named Pietro Della Valle visited Ottoman lands around 1614 and wrote in one of his letters of the fineness of the work produced by these skilled women:

Sewing of every kind is done extremely well, and far better than by us, as much by tailors with whatever clothing, as by women with linen and so forth. And they not only embroider with linen, but also with silk in various colours, on both facings, showing the same pattern back and front, and through and through. And they work with gold and silver, on the flimsiest, transparent bleached linens; and the gold in certain works, partly burnished and partly not, they make appear as if shaded, showing a certain chiaroscuro than which nothing lovelier can be seen. I have examples of this kind of work, some bought and some given me, that I am sure will be seen with pleasure and also wondered at by our ladies in Rome.[14]

METHODS

Although flax cultivation is almost non-existent today, it was prevalent in Ottoman lands until World War I. The closest region to the capital in which flax was cultivated was along the Black Sea coast of northern Anatolia, especially between Sile and Rize.[15] Before the Ottoman Empire lost most of its wealthiest and most fertile provinces in the nineteenth century, flax was obtained from both eastern and western provinces. Rumeli and Walachia were major sources. But the best quality flax was brought from Egypt. Cotton gained importance in the nineteenth century, although it had been in cultivation for centuries throughout the Anatolian peninsula.[16] Most women practicing a craft were engaged in textile production such as spinning, embroidering, and weaving. Flax as well as cotton appears to have been spun at home (fig. 5). The preferable spin direction for both flax and cotton was the Z direction. Cotton yarns were used both to weave the ground fabric and as supplementary weft yarns to create pleasing designs in an all-linen ground. Unspun silk yarns were also woven into the ground fabric, but generally as supplemental warp yarns creating stripes close to the selvedges of the fabric or as weft yarns to create horizontal banding. The material used for the ground fabric was closely associated with the type of embroidery to be executed and the function of the finished textile. For articles that were to see heavy wear-and-tear, such as large door curtains, boots, saddles, quivers, cuirasses, and tents, leather or heavier fabrics like hemp or wool were preferred. Silk ground

13 Gervers 1982, p. 20

14 Della Valle 1990, pp. 14–15

15 After World War I, the production of flax steadily dropped to a level where it was taken out of the list of agricultural products of the Republic of Turkey in the 1930s. Kandıra, Ereğli, Bartın, İnebolu, Ayancık, Sinop and Trabzon were the towns most famous for flax cultivation and the weaving of linen before the twentieth century (Keten 1969).

16 Ther 1995, p. 15

fabrics were utilized for embroidery with heavy gold threads, sequins, and pearls, as seen on *bindallı*s (dresses), slippers, and hearth covers (cat. nos. 56, 57, and 40). In the late nineteenth and early twentieth centuries, linen and cotton were preferred for light decorative household articles like *yağlık*s (napkins), *bohça*s (wrapping cloths), small or large covers and quilt covers, or small clothing articles like *uçkur*s (sashes) and *çevre*s (headscarves). The weave structure of the ground fabric was an important factor for the selection. Velvet, heavy satin weaves with thicker weft yarns, and felted woolen plain weaves were preferred

Figure 6
One of the old silk trade centers in Bursa, Koza Han, built in the 15th century

for heavy embroidery. Very loosely woven plain-weave linen ground fabrics were reserved for lighter embroidery, which utilized silk threads and a minimal amount of metallic-wrapped threads.

Ground fabrics from the sixteenth century until the early eighteenth century were generally of Z-spun, undyed linen, rarely of cotton. They were always loosely woven plain weave with no woven ornamental designs. These fabrics were narrow, between 45 and 56 cm wide, corresponding to the loom sizes of this period. For larger square and rectangular covers, such as hangings, quilt covers, turban covers, and *bohças*, several lengths of loom-width fabric were sewn together to achieve the required size. A large percentage of these textiles appear to have been embroidered before assembly. This meant that lengths of fabric were attached temporarily at first, and the designs transferred to them by means of drawing or printing. Then each length was separated and divided among several embroiderers. Each embroiderer worked on her piece at her own pace. After completion of the embroidery, the pieces were reassembled. This practice saved time but caused minor inconsistencies. As mentioned above, designs were transferred onto the fabric at the first stage of assembly. The individual motifs that created the design often started in one panel of fabric but spilled onto the neighboring one. Thus the embroiderer, when she received her commission of a single length of fabric, did not have the full design before her. Sometimes what she thought was a leaf, which she embroidered in green or blue, turned out to be part of a red blossom (cat. no. 14).

From the eighteenth century onwards, we observe a greater variety of materials and weaves. Supplemental weft or warp yarns of cotton or silk were incorporated into the ground fabrics, creating sets of repeating patterns. After the embroidery was completed, the designs woven into the ground fabric created a third layer, giving an additional vibrancy to the finished product. The weft and warp yarns seen on many of the eighteenth- and nineteenth-century linen ground fabrics were extremely fine. In the very finest examples, thread counts were approximately 40×30 per square centimeter. In previous centuries this count was generally 15×13 per square centimeter, although the linen yarns were similarly fine.

Linen ground fabric for embroidery did not show much variation in width until the end of eighteenth century. After that time wider fabrics were woven, reaching 95 cm in width, which found use in *çevres* and *bohças*. Large rectangular covers required at least three and a half fabric widths, for the *yağlık*s loom-width fabric was left uncut, while for *uçkur*s the same width of fabric was cut in half creating two equal halves (cat. nos. 4, 39, and 48).

The way the loom was set up and the ground fabric woven seemed to be the same for every type of embroidered textile, whether that fabric was destined for a *yağlık*, *bohça*, or cover. Ground fabrics for *uçkur*s, however, received a slightly different treatment during the weaving process. It appears that a calculated decision was made to weave ground fabric for *uçkur*s before the loom was set up. The widths of finished *uçkur*s generally measured around 25 cm, roughly half the loom widths of 47–55 cm seen in the widths of fabric for *yağlık*s. Their ground fabric was also woven to approximately 50 cm, but in the center, two warp yarns were placed to function as one during the set up of the loom, thus creating a distinct left and right half. If the loom was not set up for this separation and it was later decided the finished fabric should be embroidered for *uçkur*s, then a warp yarn from the center was pulled out, leaving broken warp yarns in the middle of the fabric. This separation in the fabric enabled two *uçkur*s with different designs to be embroidered on the same fabric. These double *uçkur*s were sometimes sold or kept without separating one from the other (cat. no. 52).

Luxurious silk satin weaves and silk or cotton velvets were the most expensive ground fabrics available. Valuable gold and silver thread, pearls, and semi-precious stones were applied to these costly fabrics. Textiles with satin weave and velvet ground fabrics were purchased as important items for a girl's trousseau, to represent her family's wealth and standing.

One type of ground fabric that became a flower garden in the hands of skillful Ottoman embroiderers and was admired by everyone around the world was the bath towel, *havlu* in Turkish. Although use of the term 'Turkish towel' appears in many travel books and memoirs from the nineteenth and early twentieth centuries, what was being referred to most often in these writings were *yağlık*s with a plain-weave ground fabric. For an Ottoman, the term *havlu* meant a textile with a certain kind of weave structure, which later became known as terry cloth in English. The misunderstanding perhaps started because *yağlık*s were presented to guests for the wiping of wet hands, just like a towel. Towels were generally of Z-spun undyed linen, rarely of cotton. Their weave structure was almost always 2/2 twill weave with extra-warp loop pile. Generally the extra-warp loop pile appears on the front face of the fabric, leaving the back face without pile. The placement of the pile on the fabric was usually identical. Two large bands without pile at each end were for the embroidery. An approximately 11 cm long pile band followed this plain area at both sides. The center portion of the fabric, depending on the length of the towel, was filled with another pile band (cat. nos. 45–46). The width of the towels varied from 95 cm to 64 cm and the longest ones were about 180 cm.

The best compliment an Ottoman mother could bestow upon her daughter was to call her "my silk daughter." Silk, with its softness and sheen, was a sign of luxury much sought after by people throughout history. The Ottoman city of Bursa became one of the great centers for silk trade and industry in the world (fig. 6). Its rise as an international market dates to the middle of the fourteenth century. When Bursa was a trade capital, caravans from Iran and the Far East brought large quantities of raw silk to the city each year.[17] Genoese and Florentine merchants mingled in the streets of Bursa with itinerant merchants from Iran, Damascus, and the Far East offering high prices for silk to feed the silk-crazed European élite. An embargo on all Iranian silk products after the conflict between the Ottomans and the Safavids in the sixteenth century was a major blow not only to Bursa and the Ottoman silk industry, but also to the European silk trade. During and after the seventeenth century, trade routes changed and Bursa lost its glory to other world trade centers.[18] But silk never disappeared from the lives of Bursa natives. Large orchards of mulberry trees, upon which silkworms subsist, were planted and their size increased steadily, reaching a peak in the nineteenth century, covering the plains around Bursa. Silk was a precious international commodity for the Ottoman Empire. Large portions of the raw silk arriving from the East or raised in Anatolia in towns like Bursa and Amasya were set aside for the production of silk fabrics for export until the eighteenth century. In the eighteenth and nineteenth centuries Bursa began to sell more raw silk than finished silk products. The most valuable silk threads were tightly spun, to be used for weaving the luxurious fabrics destined to become robes for the sultans and the wealthy. A portion of the unspun or loosely twisted silk yarns was marketed to embroiderers. Records of the guilds, court proceedings, and the content lists of estates from seventeenth-century Bursa indicate that there were many independent, home-based female and male silk-thread producers. These same records also indicate that there were separate silk-twister workshops, which received reeled and spun silk. Silk-twisters unwound the entire length of silk thread and drew it through loops while twisting the strands on a large twisting wheel called a *dolab*. There are no records describing the silk-spinning wheels of seventeenth-century Turkey. They probably looked like the European spinning wheels of the same period, because later in the nineteenth century Ottoman spinning wheels were very similar to European spinning wheels. They consisted of a metal tray for the raw silk and a wooden wheel.[19]

Two-plied silk threads were used in most Ottoman embroidered textiles. Both Z- and S-plied threads were sometimes used on the same textile. Embroiderers sometimes used unspun and two-plied silk embroidery threads, or highly plied and loosely plied silk embroidery threads side by side, to give dimension to the motifs they embroidered.

Cotton embroidery thread was of secondary importance to silk in the Ottoman embroidery tradition. It is almost non-existent as a surface embroidery thread. The only extensive use of it was as a couching thread in a specific style of

17 Up to 120 metric tons
18 İnalcik and Quataert 1996, pp. 218–55;
     İnalcik 1971, pp. 209–21
19 Gerber 1988, pp. 63–65

Ottoman embroidery called *dival*, a style defined by its use of metallic threads and couching.

The *kaftan*s of Sultan Süleyman's son Prince Mehmet, sashes most likely worn by chief servants of the Privy Council, and a manuscript cover, all dating to the sixteenth century, are the earliest examples of textiles in which metallic threads are used for embroidery.[20] The opening years of the eighteenth century witnessed their widespread use to enhance designs in embroidered textiles. Throughout the eighteenth century, and into the nineteenth, the use of metallic threads continued to be fashionable, increasing to the point where certain textiles were almost exclusively embroidered with them (cat. no. 35).

Metallic threads are of several types. In Ottoman embroidery, two categories may be identified: metallic-wrapped threads, and threads that are themselves metal strips or wires. Workshops for the manufacture of metallic-wrapped threads were mentioned in official Ottoman correspondence as early as the seventeenth century.[21] These metallic-wrapped threads were produced by professionals who wrapped metal strips around a silk or cotton thread, possibly with the help of a small hand-manipulated machine.[22] The wrapping direction of the metal strips appears to be predominantly Z-direction, although a few metallic-wrapped threads wrapped in S-direction have been observed. The color of the core thread was selected to enhance the intended effect. Yellow silk threads were used for metal strips of gold or gold alloy. These threads were known as *klaptan* or *klapdan* in Turkish. Light-yellow silk threads are seen more frequently in embroidered textiles dating from before the late nineteenth century. Dark-yellow silk threads were used more often towards the end of the nineteenth century. White silk threads were used as core thread for metal strips of silver or dipped into silver.

Metal strips and wires are more frequently encountered in nineteenth-century embroidery. *Tırtıl* or *tertıl* (metal wire spirals) were utilized mostly in *dival* embroidery accompanying the metal wire couching. As in *tırtıl*, sequins and pearls were added as secondary elements to highlight the designs. On rare occasions a textile was embroidered solely with secondary or accessory embroidery materials such as metal sequins, as seen in a round *nihali* made for use in serving coffee, now in The Textile Museum's collections (cat. no. 41).

A *gergef* was a rectangular embroidery frame standing on four stubby legs. It looked like a short, small table (fig. 5). Some were beautifully carved; others were decorated with inlaid mother-of-pearl. Each part of the frame could easily be detached, thus making it easy to carry and store. Before starting her work, the

20 Delibaş 1987, p. 48
21 Gerber 1988, p. 113
22 For further discussion on metallic yarns
   see Farr 1994, pp. 65–85, and Ellis 1992,
   pp. 37–39

first task of the embroiderer was to stretch a ground fabric on this frame with the help of another fabric called *gergef* cloth and strings. The fabric to be embroidered was sewn onto the *gergef* cloth from the narrow ends. The strings attached to the *gergef* cloth were then threaded through the holes on the frame and pulled so as to stretch the ground fabric as tight as possible. The embroiderer sat cross-legged in front of the *gergef*, which was placed either on the floor or on the *divan*. She kept her right hand above and the left hand below the frame, working the needle up and down very fast.[23]

Another frame used for embroidery was a round hoop called a *kasnak*. These round frames could be quite large in size. The embroidery fabric was stretched on it, also with the help of strings. The fabric was sometimes stretched so much that when tapped, it gave a sound. To start embroidering, the embroiderer sat on the *divan* and held the *kasnak* between her or his chest and the back of the *divan*, with the hands left free. The embroiderer would hold the silk thread in the left hand underneath the *kasnak* and the *kasnak tığ* (kasnak needle) in the right hand above it.[24]

Dival embroidery was done either in workshops, or by professional embroiderers at home. It was sometimes referred to as *maraş işi*, after the town of Maraş in southeastern Turkey, where embroiderers excelled in this kind of workmanship. This embroidery required large equipment and strength. The stand used was called a *cülde*. A *çağ* (spool holder) and *biz* (sharp needle) to punch holes for the threaded needle to pass through were crucial to the process. A *cülde* is like a pair of giant tweezers, which clasps the ground fabric between its arms. The thick ground fabric had to be secured and stationary to permit the embroiderer to push the needle hard through the thick fabric. There were small stands for homes and large stands for workshops. *Dival* embroidery required an investment both in material and skill not everyone was willing to make. Thus textiles with *dival* embroidery were produced by professionals and purchased in the bazaars. Household items or garments embroidered with *dival* embroidery were expensive and special attention was given to their care. They were taken out rarely, and passed on from one generation to another (cat. nos. 22, 42, 56, and 57).[25]

Simple needles made out of bone, tusk, or metal were the basic tools for all types of embroidery, whether using silk threads or metallic-wrapped threads. The sizes of the needles and their holes were selected according to the diameter of the thread to be used. When metallic-wrapped threads were used, larger needle holes were required. Teardrop-shaped flat needles were used for metal strips. These needles had two holes for the strip to pass through, to return over itself

23 Sürür 1976, p. 33
24 Sürür 1976, p. 33; Yüksel 1997, pp. 377–80
25 Yüksel 1997, pp. 356–76

and be secured. The hook for embroidery that used *kasnak*s (round frames) consisted of a curved metal needle with a wooden pear-shaped handle. The metal part of the needle resembled a crochet needle with a hooked end. The pear shape of the handle provided an easy grip for the embroiderer. These hooks came in several sizes and lengths to accommodate different types of ground fabric and embroidery threads.[26] Embroiderers used three other items for their comfort. A *tırnak* was a loop with a fingernail-shaped piece attached. It allowed the embroiderer to stretch the thread better as well as protecting the embroiderer's finger. A *ciğerdeldi* was a sharp implement, approximately 7 cm long, made of bone or tusk. Wider in the center than at the edges, it allowed the embroiderer to create holes in thick fabric or leather for inserting embroidery threads. An *iğnedan* was a small box where all embroidery tools were kept except the *gergef* and the *kasnak*.[27]

Designs were transferred onto the ground fabric by one of several methods. In one of the methods the pattern sample was an embroidered textile made previously; its motifs were copied by counting the warp and weft elements of the ground fabric and inserting embroidery threads in corresponding places in the new fabric. This method of copying required a ground cloth with a similar weave structure, and similar warp and weft counts. This type of design transfer was most often used at home to copy older materials passed down through generations. It offered a means of securing the continuity of the family design traditions.

Another method of design transfer, used primarily at home, was to use charcoal dust. A design was first drawn on paper, which was then pricked with a needle. Little holes were punched all along the outlines of the motif. Then the paper was placed on the ground fabric with a bagful of mashed charcoal, which was pressed on the paper. The charcoal dust slipped through the holes to transfer the motif to the fabric.[28]

In the workshops, where output was larger, a more frequently used method of transferring designs was to draw them on the ground fabric. This was done either freehand with brushes or an inking pen, or with the help of templates or print blocks. Generally a professional design draftsman was the person to apply this method. Templates and print blocks were used to transfer the outlines of the motifs onto the fabric. This method allowed the same motif to be used repeatedly on the same textile or on more than one textile.[29] Some of the larger textiles, such as wall and quilt covers, and *bohça*s, were decorated with overall repeat patterning in ogival lattices or ascending meanders using this method of design transfer. These templates or blocks generally carried a single motif. Two or more of these

26 Sürür 1976, p. 33
27 *Ibid.*
28 *Ibid.*, p. 48
29 Sürür 1976, p. 48; Ther 1995, p. 18

were required to create the overall repeat patterns seen on the textiles (cat. nos. 4 and 6). Sometimes a combination of freehand drawing and block patterns can be observed on these textiles. One of the best examples is in The Textile Museum collection. It is a large cover with ascending branches (cat. no. 14). It appears that the branches were drawn freehand, but other motifs were transferred onto the fabric by means of blocks or templates.

Figure 8
Çintemani *motif (three balls and two wavy lines). Detail from The Textile Museum 1.8 (cat. no. 6)*

Figure 7
Dival *embroidery. Detail from The Textile Museum 1962.46.1 (cat. no. 22)*

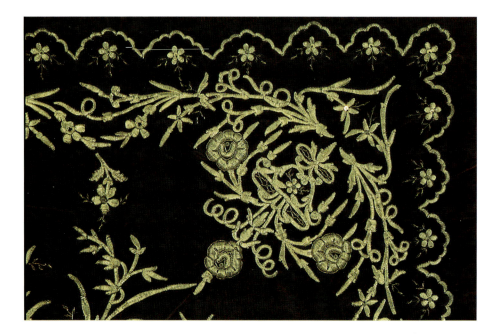

Terms describing Ottoman embroidery styles, techniques, and stitches are so intermingled that to separate them is almost impossible. The confusion is mainly caused by the way the embroiderers themselves used the terms. Most often a term refers at the same time to a style and a technique, or to a technique and a stitch, or to a style and a stitch. *Dival* embroidery was the major Ottoman embroidery style.[30] The two main materials used for *dival* embroidery are metallic and cotton threads (fig. 7). The embroidery technique used is couching. The initial preparation for this style of embroidery was especially involved. After drawing and redrawing designs on different types of paper, in the final stage they were drawn onto cardboard and then cut out with a special knife called a *möhlüke* (*keski*). The cutout design was pasted over the ground fabric with special glue. Then the ground fabric and the lining were clamped to a *cülde*. The embroider-

30 The term 'embroidery style' describes a type of embroidery often identified by characteristic techniques, embroidery stitches or colors and yarns used. Embroidery style defines any type of embroidery specific to a culture or time period (The Lloyd Cotsen Textile Documentation Project, The Textile Museum 1998).

ers worked by holding the metallic threads in their left hand, with a sharp needle and the cotton couching thread in their right hand. A group of four to five metallic threads reeled from the spool holder was moved from side to side above the fabric across the cutout pattern. At each pass, the cotton thread was brought out from beneath the fabric through a hole opened by the sharp needle. This couching thread secured the metallic threads on the side of the cutout design. This process was continued back and forth until the entire cutout design was covered. *Tırtıl* (metal wire spirals), sequins, and pearls were added later to enhance the design.[31]

Anavata, a less expensive version of *dival* embroidery, utilized thick cotton or silk threads in place of metal wires and is found in textiles from the end of the eighteenth and throughout the nineteenth century.[32]

Zerdüz embroidery is another Ottoman embroidery style, similar to *dival*. A gold or silver wire, or a braid, was laid out on the surface of the ground fabric in a pattern and secured by stitches worked from below the fabric at frequent intervals with a similar color thread.[33]

Both *tel kırma*- and *tel kakma*-style embroidery used metal strips and a flat needle. What distinguishes them from one another is the different stitches used. In *tel kırma* embroidery, short metal strips were wrapped around a counted number of warp and weft yarns and then secured. Loosely woven ground fabrics were preferred for this style of embroidery. *Tel kakma* utilized longer metal strips with the same stitches as seen in silk embroidery. Thus *tel kakma* and other lighter silk embroideries share similar fabrics of a plain woven ground.[34]

The majority of terms used in Ottoman embroidery refer either to the technique or to the stitch used. Counted work, pattern darning, couching, pulled work, and tambour work were the most important techniques used.[35]

Hesap işi was the Turkish term for 'counted work.' This embroidery technique was used on the majority of embroidered textiles from the Ottoman period.[36] Counted work is done by counting the warp and weft yarns of a ground fabric with an even weave. In Ottoman embroidery, silk metallic-wrapped threads and metal strips were embroidered on linen fabric with a balanced plain-weave ground. The fineness of the embroidery depended on the fineness of the ground weave. Although the stitch repertory of Ottoman *hesap işi* is limited to a few very simple stitches, the ways in which these stitches were manipulated are almost innumerable. This technique and certain design features such as a preference for a few distinct floral motifs such as the tulip and the hyacinth make Ottoman

31 Yüksel 1997, pp. 356–76
32 Sürür 1976, p. 41
33 *Ibid*.
34 Yüksel 1997, pp. 347–55
35 'Embroidery technique' is a guide term for embroidery processes. It defines different types of work, with different actions being performed upon the ground fabric (The Lloyd Cotsen Textile Documentation Project, The Textile Museum 1998).
36 Sürür 1976, pp. 36–39

embroidery different and instantly recognizable from other embroideries from around the world. *Hesap işi* can be divided into two groups, termed for the sake of simplification double-sided and single-sided *hesap işi*. Stitches such as the double running stitch used in the double-sided *hesap işi* created a similar appearance on both sides of the ground fabric, making it possible for the viewer to enjoy both sides of the textile. In single-sided *hesap işi*, stitches such as the running stitch created an effect that could be viewed from one side of the fabric only. *İnce iş* (slender or thin work) was a variation of *hesap işi*, but the warp and weft counting of the stitch used in this technique was so fine that the designs appeared to be woven in, instead of embroidered.

Pattern-darning technique is a method of disposing running stitches as a filling to create one or more patterns (fig. 8). The running stitch used in the Ottoman pattern-darning technique was always counted and each row was diagonally aligned. This technique was favored up until the mid-eighteenth century.

In the simplest terms, couching involved laying an embroidery thread on one face of the fabric and securing it by introducing a second thread from beneath the fabric. *Dival* and *zerdüz* are the major embroidery styles that utilize couching. Sometimes the same yarn could function both as the couched thread and the couching thread: such an embroidery technique is known as self-couching. Romanian and Bukharan stitches were the two stitches preferred in Ottoman embroidery for the self-couching technique. *Atma* is the Turkish term that refers both to the technique of couching and to a specific composite stitch used in the couching technique. *Atma* is more frequently encountered in earlier Ottoman embroidered textiles dating from the late seventeenth to the late eighteenth century (fig. 9).

Pulled work, which was popular from the early nineteenth century onwards, was produced by pulling the warp and weft yarns of a ground fabric out of alignment and holding them in place with embroidery stitches under tension. This created holes or spaces in or between the woven elements of the ground fabric. Different embroidery stitches were used in this technique to achieve the desired perforated look.

Kasnak işi (tambour work) takes its name from the frame it uses. In this technique, it is very rare to see any stitch other than chain stitch being used (fig. 10). Neither metal strips nor metallic-wrapped thread were applied. *Kasnak işi* was generally practiced in workshops. Small or large covers, especially round floor spreads, barber robes, hangings, and prayer cloths were produced using this technique (cat. nos. 43, 44).[37]

37 Yüksel 1997, pp. 377–80

Figure 9
Atma *stitch. Detail from*
The Textile Museum 1.7
(cat. no. 20)

The stitches used in Ottoman embroidery can be divided into two groups, reversible and non-reversible stitches. Non-reversible stitches were more frequently used on textiles dating from before the mid-eighteenth century. The running stitch, the *atma* stitch, the triangular or Turkish stitch, the chain stitch, the herringbone stitch, the Romanian self-couching stitch, and the Bukharan self-couching stitch are in this group. In Ottoman embroidery, the running stitch, used in the pattern-darning technique to fill large design areas, was disposed in closely worked parallel rows in diagonal alignment (fig. 8). *Kum iğnesi* (sand stitch) was the name given to this stitch in Turkish. Stitches are not equal in length on the front face and the reverse. The embroiderer generally counted three yarns, inserted the needle, and came out again after counting one yarn. The count sometimes went up to five yarns and came down to one yarn, in which case the stitches were equal length on both sides of the fabric, giving the appearance of being woven into the fabric rather than embroidered.[38] This stitch might have been the extremely delicate stitch rejected by the women embroiderers in the

Figure 10
Kasnak işi. *Detail from*
The Textile Museum
1985.48.1a (cat. no. 43)

38 A large cover (TSM 31/4) in Topkapı
   Palace Museum's collection is the best-
   known example of this type of stitch.

Figure 11
Composite stitch. Detail
from The Textile
Museum 1.31 (cat. no.
27)

Figure 12
Turkish stitch. Detail
from The Textile
Museum 1.13 (cat. no. 15)

Topkapı Palace letter.[39] The working direction of the running stitch changed frequently, not only from one fabric to another, but on the same fabric from one motif to another. Embroiderers easily switched from embroidering in the warp direction to embroidering in the weft direction. There seems to be no relationship between switching directions and trying to create a different texture. The only guiding principle appears to be not to switch the stitching direction while working on the same motif. The running stitch is generally associated with earlier textiles. Large covers and *bohça*s dating from before the end of the eighteenth century seem to be the only textiles in which this stitch is used exclusively.

The *atma* stitch was a combination of two stitches (fig. 9). It was sometimes known as the Oriental stitch and worked in two steps.[40] The whole motif was covered working a single-faced satin stitch using unspun silk in the first step. In the second step, a plied silk thread was laid over the first layer of threads at a ninety-degree angle, and secured by self-couching using the Bukharan stitch.

Another composite stitch, the name of which is unknown to us today, utilized a double running stitch with a Romanian self-couching stitch in alternate rows (fig. 11). Both stitches were worked diagonal to the weave. Sometimes the Romanian self-couching stitch was replaced by a double running stitch done in steps rather than a straight line (cat. nos. 28–29). This composite stitch was not as widely used as the running stitch (cat. no. 27) and seems to have been forgotten by the mid-eighteenth century.

The chain stitch was mostly applied in *kasnak işi* embroidery (tambour work) of the late eighteenth and nineteenth centuries (fig. 10). In the seventeenth and eighteenth centuries, this stitch was utilized to create thin borders for main design fields. In the chain stitch, the thread was caught with a hook inserted from above the ground fabric and pulled through, creating a loop; this loop was then secured again with a second loop pulled through slightly beyond the first.[41]

The double running stitch, the satin stitch, and the *muşabak* stitch are the most frequently used stitches from the group of reversible stitches. The double running stitch, along with the running stitch from the non-reversible group, formed the backbone of Ottoman embroidery. Ottoman embroiderers manipulated these two stitches in innumerable ways and forms to create many pleasing results. Embroiderers were often able to fill large surfaces and outline motifs using only these two stitches.

The double running stitch is the hallmark of embroidered textiles from the eighteenth century onwards (fig. 13).[42] It decorated many textiles eagerly purchased and lovingly kept by European travelers, as well as those treasured by the

39 See note 9, pp. 30–31
40 Dillmont 1978, p. 166
41 Yüksel 1997, pp. 377–80
42 Thomas 1954, pp. 117, 121–22; Emery 1994,
    p. 235

Ottomans. This stitch, like the running stitch, was used as a filling stitch and required counting the warp and weft elements of the ground fabric. When used for outlining, it was named *gözeme*. As a filling stitch, it was referred to as *pesent*. There were other parts of designs where a double running stitch created a stepped effect, such as flower branches with long, narrow forms. When used in that manner, the double running stitch was termed *hesap işi iğne* (counted work stitch).

Although the same stitch may have been used for the different areas in an embroidered design, the various ways it was applied produced different effects for the viewer. Thus the confusion of embroidery style, technique, and stitch names. There were many names given to these different effects, although the stitch stayed the same. A double running stitch disposed in closely worked parallel rows in diagonal alignment created diagonal lines, while the same stitch worked in straight alignment created horizontal lines. Working the same double running stitch straight or in steps diagonal to the weave of the ground fabric created totally different effects. The reason Ottoman embroiderers favored this stitch may be because it was an easy stitch to manipulate to achieve different effects, and it looked almost identical on both sides of the ground fabric when the embroidery was complete.

Another stitch frequently seen, which showed similar characteristics of an identical effect on both sides of the fabric, was the satin stitch. A companion to the double running stitch, they were often used together. While the double running stitch was used to fill large roses and pomegranates, the satin stitch was reserved for creating the stems for flowers and flowing ribbons of bouquets.

Muşabak (*müşebbek*) and *mürver* are the names of two stitches used for pulled work. *Mürver* might have been an addition to the Ottoman stitch repertory at the end of the nineteenth century.[43] *Muşabak* gave the same appearance on both sides of the fabric, while *mürver* had a distinct front face and back face. *Muşabak* is a combination of the reverse faggot and single faggot stitches (fig. 13).[44] *Mürver*, although worked differently, created a similar netted effect. The size of the holes created on the ground fabric by these two stitches depended on how loosely the fabric was woven and the strength the embroiderer applied during the embroidery process. If the embroidery was worked on a loosely woven ground and the embroiderer pulled her threads tightly during the stitching, she would create a netted effect. If she preferred to work without pulling tightly, the work would not have a perforated appearance.

The triangular two-sided stitch or Turkish stitch is worked in diagonal to the ground fabric over counted threads (fig. 12).[45] This stitch does not give a true reversible effect and seems to have been forgotten by the nineteenth century. The other frequently used stitch was the fishbone stitch, which gives a double-sided effect. It was usually applied to flower stems or leaves.

When examined carefully, most of the stitches used in Ottoman embroidery to create reversibility were the stitches that required being worked first in one direction and then in the same manner in the reverse direction on top of the first

43 Ellis 1989, pp. 138–40
44 Thomas 1954, pp. 91–92; Ellis 1989, p. 139
45 Dillmont 1978, pp. 97–98; Thomas 1954, pp. 203–04

stitching. The double running stitch, the Turkish stitch, the fishbone stitch, and the *muşabak* stitch belong to this group of stitches.

In Ottoman embroidery, except for certain pulled-work stitches, most stitches were in circulation from the seventeenth century onwards. The only difference between earlier work and later work was how many types of stitches were used on a single ground fabric. The seventeenth- and eighteenth-century embroiderers generally limited their selection to one or two types of stitch for each work (cat. no. 5); in the nineteenth and early twentieth centuries, it was customary to use three or four different stitches on a single fabric (cat. no. 54).

Red, blue, green, yellow, white, and black/brown were the six colors used most frequently in Ottoman embroidery from the seventeenth to the mid-eighteenth century. Among these colors, black was used for the outlining of white motifs or for very minor highlighting. Each motif was represented with a single bold basic color and did not require highlights or shading. From the middle of the eighteenth century into the nineteenth, the Ottoman color repertoire for embroidery threads expanded. Using the six basic colors in single tones was no longer enough, and shades of each color were sought. Some embroideries were made with ten to fifteen colors, including several shades of the basic six. Black outlines were no longer used; embroiderers were able to use lighter or darker shades of the same color thread for outlines as the thread used for the motif. Strong colors waned, while pastel tones such as pinks, light blues, light greens, and soft browns became fashionable in the eighteenth and nineteenth centuries.

Changes in the Ottoman political, military, commercial, and cultural spheres profoundly affected the lives of Ottoman subjects. Openness to Western cultures brought new ideas, new customs, and new fashions. Ottoman embroidery changed like everything else. Embroidery was an art form produced by a large portion of the population, both commercially and domestically, and the finished product was an inextricable part of Ottoman daily life. From the early eighteenth century onwards, more art objects, books, and engravings changed hands between the Ottomans and the Europeans, with both sides eager to learn more about each other's lives and arts. European horticultural books with accurately portrayed flowers, design books with architectural drawings, oil paintings, and books on embroidery and weaving design and method made their way to the Ottoman lands. The spread of these new ideas quickly advanced in the hands of skilled Ottoman craftsmen who were eager to try new designs and colors, although they never relinquished the old ways of doing things.

The most recognizable change in embroidered textiles during this period is their color palette. Bold designs with a limited color palette in the seventeenth and early eighteenth centuries were replaced by small designs with subdued colors created by soft pastel tones. Shading by using several tones of the same color on a single motif created a perception of three-dimensionality. In previous centuries a sense of depth was created by layering motifs. The introduction of new stitches and the use of more than one type of stitch in embroidered textiles created contrasting surface textures, which reflected a desire to show richness and three-dimensionality in the European manner. In the late nineteenth century, using only a few stitches to create a luxurious three-dimensional effect was no longer enough. Embroidery became sculptural and enriched by the addition of *tırtıl*, pearls, sequins, gold and silver metal strips, and metallic-wrapped threads.

The swelling number of newly wealthy and educated bureaucrats in this later period were eager to follow the lead of the Palace. They wanted to imitate everything the Palace used and were willing to pay any sum to the craftsmen who could replicate Palace work. Many richly embroidered textiles, as well as other art objects, found new places, not in the Palace treasury, but in private houses in İstanbul and large city centers like Bursa, İzmir, Cairo, and Damascus. The Palace played a role as critical in the development of Ottoman decorative arts in this period as it had in the past. In Ottoman culture, change was most often introduced from the court. The eighteenth and nineteenth centuries comprised a period in which the Ottoman court sought to remake itself in the fashion of a European court. The court was keen to adopt the customs and costumes of European culture. Craftsmen quickly copied for the İstanbul élite whatever was produced in this period for the Palace under the influence of European art. These objects were then carried to the provinces where they were widely promoted by İstanbul-educated bureaucrats.

Designs and Functions

Skill of the hand
Glory of the eye[1]

DESIGNS AND COMPOSITIONS OF OTTOMAN EMBROIDERED TEXTILES

To achieve a systematic classification of Ottoman-style embroidered textiles, looking at them by design and function offers a useful approach. Compositions and individual motifs employed on embroidered textiles are similar to those depicted in other media. The freedom offered by embroidery as a medium allows for more individual expression, a factor which can sometimes make comparison with other arts difficult. The creators of these embroidered textiles had more freedom in executing the designs than did other kinds of craftsmen under the strict control of an imperial workshop.

Motifs and their composition for a textile woven on a drawloom have to be decided before weaving can begin; during the weaving process weavers repeat the same motif, row after row, until the whole fabric is woven. In embroidery there is generally more flexibility for the design draftsman or the embroiderer to manipulate both the individual motifs and the overall composition. The same motifs and compositions even come out differently when made by different hands. This factor facilitated the development of a wide variety of compositions, each with a repertoire of differently executed motifs with slight variations.[2]

Embroidery from the seventeenth to the eighteenth century shows preferences for clear forms, distinct compositions with a defined direction, precisely rendered motifs, and a small number of bold colors. Designs on large textiles, such as covers, *bohça*s, and turban covers show a close affinity to woven fabrics from the same period. Embroidered textiles before the mid-eighteenth century were composed of one or two motifs combined with interconnected elements such as a lattice to form a large, flowing pattern covering the entire surface area of the fabric. These compositions had three important characteristics:

1. Every composition was framed with a border, regardless of the shape of the ground fabric, thus creating two parts to the composition: a central field and a border. The border could be narrow or wide; wider ones were decorated with floral scrolls that were usually a simplified version of the motifs used in the main field (cat. no. 16).

2. The overall design in the central field was an infinitely repeating pattern, which created the illusion that the design continued beyond the framing borders (cat. no. 6).

Opposite:
Cover fragment, 17th century. Detail from The Textile Museum 1.41 (cat. no. 5)

---

1 Turkish proverb: *el emeği, göz nuru.*
2 Several covers with designs almost identical to those on The Textile Museum 1.8 and 1982.40.3 (cat. nos. 4–6) are published in Erber 1995, pp. 206–07, cat. no. s2/5 and pp. 210–15, cat. nos. s3/2/1, s3/2/2, s3/2/3. Another cover similar to The Textile Museum 1982.40.3 is in the Topkapı Palace collection (TSM 3/1807).

3. Floral motifs and compositions were often stylized in appearance. Although certain flowers were depicted naturally enough to be identifiable, the ways they were put together were entirely artificial, as on one of The Textile Museum covers (cat. no. 3). Leaves, tulips, carnations, and pomegranates can easily be picked out in this crowded design, but the way they are drawn does not fit any natural organic form.

Figure 14
Textile fragment, 16th century. The Textile Museum 1.68. Acquired by George Hewitt Myers in 1952

Each design consists of a large main motif with smaller secondary motifs. The placement of the main motif repeats several times in the central field, dictating the overall layout. Motifs on a single row can be arranged in diagonal alignment with motifs in the preceding row, which creates an ogival layout, or they can be placed in straight alignment. Sometimes a visible lattice was added to the layout (cat. no. 12). Among the early large textiles dating from the seventeenth and the eighteenth centuries, an ogival layout for the overall design was favored. The ground surrounding the main motifs was filled with secondary motifs (cat. no. 4). The addition of a visible lattice created a foreground and a background in the composition, lending the playfulness that is so characteristic of Ottoman art (cat. nos. 4, 5, 6, 11, 12, and 13). Secondary motifs in the composition also contributed to this visual play (cat. nos. 7 and 8). Often the overall composition and individual motifs are composed of many secondary motifs. These often obscure the boundaries of a single motif. A composition called 'ascending leaves', for example, is composed of three or four parallel meandering bands with alternating different blossoms, facing left or right at regular intervals (cat. no. 14). This composition was also favored for woven textiles (fig. 14).

In another composition in Ottoman embroidered textiles, the motifs are placed in straight alignment (cat. nos. 7, 8, 9, 15, 20, and 21). Although this composition might at first appear rigid, the sinuous and curvilinear Ottoman floral motifs break the rigidity to create playful and flowing compositions (cat. nos. 7, 9, and 15). Circular compositions were utilized for textiles that were round in shape, or for those square or rectangular in shape but intended to be viewed from four sides (cat. nos. 2, 17, 18, and 29). This type of circular composition generally has a small circular center in the form of a rosette containing an inner floral motif similar to the main motifs. The main motifs seem to grow out of the corners and edges and point towards the center.

Ottomans loved flowers, so floral forms and designs are common in Ottoman decorative arts. Their interest in flowers led to manuscripts and albums specially written with illustrations for individual plants in mind.[3] Flower-filled medallions and blossoms placed in large ogival lattices are the most frequently encountered motifs in embroidered textiles. Among the flowers, fruits, and leaves revered by the Ottomans, tulips, carnations, hyacinths, pomegranates, and the leaves of the Oriental plane tree were most often used for design inspiration from the sixteenth to the early eighteenth century. Large serrated leaves, huge blossoms, *çintemani*s (three balls and two wavy lines), and cloud bands are other motifs frequently seen on embroidered textiles from this period. The decisions as to which motifs to embroider appear to have been made by the embroiderer without regard to the shape or function of the finished product. Thus the same motifs are shared by many textiles with different functions (cat. nos. 15, 17, 27, and 47).

Medallions or shields with a bold look appeared in Ottoman art at the end of the sixteenth century.[4] But they were never used alone in Ottoman embroidered textiles or in Ottoman art in general. Rather they serve as a background for floral motifs. A clustering effect creates a much-loved sense of layering (cat. no. 4).

The Ottoman standard for a tulip required that the flower be of almond shape, medium-sized with a long stem, and with extremely long, sharply pointed, and deeply serrated petals of gorgeous coloring (fig. 15).[5] The reign of Ahmed III

3   Titley 1979, p. 33
4   Denny 1982, p. 135
5   Mansel 1995, p. 166

(1718–1730) was the famous *Lâle Devri* (Tulip Period) during which a passion for the acquisition and cultivation of tulips swept the Ottoman Empire and spread to Europe. This craze for tulips created a new phrase, 'Tulipomania' in English. The Sultan and the wealthy İstanbul élite competed with each other, spending fortunes to outdo each other in the splendor of their homes and gardens, particularly on rare and beautiful tulip bulbs. The tulip as a motif sometimes played a major role, sometimes a secondary role, but it was ever-present on embroidered textiles from the sixteenth to the eighteenth century (cat. nos. 4 and 10). In some instances the tulip motif shared an equal level of importance with other motifs (cat. no. 16). While the tulip and its many varieties were much loved in this period, it lost favor to the rose in the late eighteenth and nineteenth centuries.[6]

The hyacinth remained one of the most favored motifs in Ottoman embroidery until the turn of the twentieth century, although it always played a secondary role in designs. The hyacinth is the object of a particularly fine early eighteenth-century manuscript, the *Sümbülname* (An Ode to the Hyacinth).[7] The reason for their long-lasting reign might have been that hyacinths were also favored as sweet-smelling flowers in the garden. Their care was easier than the capricious tulip's. They were often grown in boxes outside the windows of Ottoman houses, spreading their sweet smell into the rooms (fig. 16).

6   Gürsü 1988, p. 182; Ther 1995, pp. 21–22
7   Tansuğ 1988, pp. 56–72, *Sümbülname,*
    The Topkapı Palace Museum Library
    (Hazine # 414)

The carnation fascinated designers with its many-layered petals. It appears in many works of Ottoman art, sometimes as a large motif and sometimes as a smaller secondary motif. The carnation, usually portrayed in profile, is always recognizable by its fan-like head (fig. 18).[8]

Arched flower branches give embroidery designs a sense of movement even if the layout is rigid (fig. 17). This floral motif is sometimes depicted with a secondary smaller branch as well as with different blossoms in a stylized grouping, but the placement of the blossoms on the branch stays the same (cat. nos. 15, 17, 21, 27, 28, and 47).

Three other motifs should be mentioned among the favorites of Ottoman embroidery: the pomegranate, the *çintemani*, and the crown. The pomegranate is a secondary motif in Ottoman embroidered textiles and plays a role similar to that of the hyacinth. It is depicted with a three-pointed little crown above the seeds inside (fig. 19).[9] The *çintemani* is a motif consisting of three balls placed in a triangular arrangement accompanied by two or three parallel wavy lines. Occasionally, the three balls and wavy lines are used separately (fig. 8).[10] The crown motif appeared to enter the Ottoman repertoire around the beginning of the sixteenth century (fig. 20). Italian fabrics imported into the Ottoman Empire or the desire to appeal to European tastes for exported textiles are thought to

8   Gürsü 1988, p. 182; Ther 1995, p. 21
9   Gürsü 1988, pp. 182–83
10 *Ibid.*, p. 180

have influenced the creation of this crown motif. In the archival materials, the motif itself is generally referred to as a 'foreign' motif.[11] it generally occupied a secondary role in overall design layout and was often used at the points of intersection in a lattice (cat. no. 6).

For the Ottoman embroiderer, besides well-balanced compositions and well-executed motifs, color was crucial to complete the work and to achieve the desired bold and eye-pleasing effects. Very few colors were employed until the early eighteenth century. Red, green, blue, white, and yellow were used for motifs. Brown or black was used for outlining. Even with this limited palette, embroiderers were able to combine colors to create vibrant and colorful compositions (cat. no. 3).

Interest in European art and technology, beginning in the early eighteenth century, spread rapidly in the second half of the century and continued through the nineteenth. Gifts of art objects, books, and drawings, as well as ideas brought back from France by Ambassador Yirmisekiz (Çelebi) Mehmed Efendi, steadily influenced design concepts in Ottoman art. As Ottoman artists combined designs and motifs from the exciting new style called European Rococo with the older classical Ottoman style, they created a new style later termed Ottoman or Turkish Rococo. After this first strong contact, many books, magazines, and drawings brought in from European capitals became choice objects to purchase in the

11 Erber 1995, p. 66; Gürsü 1988, p. 183

bazaars. More literature appeared; more people read; and many ideas were exchanged. Changes in the culture and the lifestyle of the Ottomans are clearly reflected in embroidered textiles, which embellished their everyday lives.

After the mid-eighteenth century, compositions on embroidered textiles began to change as well. Overall repeat designs with ogival or 'ascending leaves' layouts seemed to lose favor. The overall repeat with straight alignment remained in favor and was used exclusively for small rectangular embroidered textiles called mirror covers. The characteristic of this layout is that the motifs change their direction in the middle of the composition (cat. nos. 19 and 29). Circular compositions continued to be applied in the late eighteenth and nineteenth centuries. Individual motifs became smaller and divided into small sections. Except for a few small items with overall repeat patterns, the majority of textiles were embroidered around the edges or at two narrow ends with same corresponding motifs facing in opposite directions (cat. nos. 23 and 30). This allowed the design to appear right side up when hung from its center on a person's arm or around a maiden's waist.

Designs from the late eighteenth century onwards can generally be divided into two parts: a major and a minor band. Motifs used in the minor band were usually an adaptation in miniature of major band motifs. If the embroidery was done

Figure 20
Crown. Detail from The Textile Museum 1.8 (cat. no 6)

around the perimeter of the textile, it was enlivened with additional large motifs at the four corners (cat. nos. 23–26).

Flowers remained the most prominent elements in the composition of Ottoman embroidered textiles as well as in the other decorative arts from the second half of the eighteenth century into the nineteenth. Floral sprigs of the eighteenth century gradually became the lavish floral sprays or flower bouquets of the nineteenth century under the influence of European Rococo (cat. nos. 19 and 45). Large motifs of flower and leaf garlands were enhanced with metallic threads and became more exuberant (cat. nos. 30, 38, and 39). While the repertory of floral motifs continued to expand, representations of these motifs also changed, becoming more and more natural in appearance. One of the most common motifs from this period was a flower bouquet of small flowers, twigs, a large rose, and a hyacinth branch arching above it (cat. no. 46). Charles White, who lived in İstanbul between 1842 and 1844, mentioned in his book a similar bouquet when discussing the importance of flowers and gardens to the Ottomans:

Sending a basket containing a ripe pomegranate garnished with a single blossom of hyacinth, a marigold, and twig of cypress, surmounted by a full blown rose, held together with a silken thread means "Model of earthly affection! My heart burns for

*Figure 21
Columns and arches.
Detail from The Textile
Museum 1983.59.9 (cat.
no. 34)*

*Figure 22
Grapes. Detail from The
Textile Museum
1983.59.8 (cat. no. 37)*

thee with undying constancy. Queen of my fate! Oh take pity on my anguish, or the mournful cypress will soon weave over my untimely grave.[12]

A vase with a large spray of flowers started to appear in both pictorial and textile arts around this time (cat. nos. 32, 50–53). This flower vase motif might have been an attempt to put the earlier floral sprig motif into a more naturalistic environment (cat. nos. 29, 47, and 48). Oriental plane trees, weeping willows, and palm trees began to accompany the lone cypress tree of the seventeenth and early eighteenth centuries. Many fruit motifs appear, including grapes and melons, alongside pomegranates (fig. 22). This period also marked the introduction of landscape designs depicting scenery and architectural features generally related to gardens. Arcades, arches and columns were employed as dividers for floral motifs (fig. 21). Shores with *yalıs*, mosques, *mescids* (small prayer halls) and *türbes* (tombs) with surrounding gardens, pleasure tents on the hillsides, and ships sailing are all new additions to an expanding repertory of motifs (fig. 12). With simple scenes, embroiderers started to experiment with perspective. Their first, instinctive way of achieving this was by putting one motif behind another, or by raising one motif above the others (cat. nos. 33, 34, and 35).

12 White 1845, pp. 308–09

Figure 23
Wall tiles, Court of the Haremağaları (*Black eunuchs*), *Topkapı Palace Harem, İstanbul*

Figure 24
Tombstone, Muradiye Külliyesi, Bursa

Figure 25 (right)
Wall tiles, mausoleum of Prince Mustafa, Muradiye Külliyesi, Bursa

Color was a key component of the softer style appearing in the later eighteenth century. Sometimes, in a single embroidered textile, fifteen or more shades of color can be counted. The colors selected were increasingly pastel tones. Several shades of the same color were applied to create the effect of shading. By using two tones of the same color, embroiderers could create lighter and darker sections in a single motif, suggesting depth. Embroiderers began using gold and silver metallic threads extensively in their work to create a gilded effect synonymous with the Rococo style. Sometimes they almost went so far as to employ only metallic threads in their work (cat. no. 35). At other times, metallic threads were applied to highlight certain parts of a motif or a design (fig. 21).

Designs on embroidered textiles from the earliest to the latest periods reflect what was practiced in the broader range of Ottoman art, although embroidery as a medium allowed for more individual expression. Both compositions and motifs were shared out among Ottoman artists and craftsman working in different media (cat. nos. 4 and 14, and figs. 14, 23, and 25). *Nakkaşhane* (the royal design atelier) appeared to be the source of the design pool where new designs were created, distributed to various craftsmen, and subsequently rendered in several media, including textiles. Sharing compositions and motifs among artists and craftsman continued in the nineteenth century (cat. nos. 37 and 50, and figs. 24 and 26). Wall paintings began to replace wall tiles in fashionable Ottoman homes, following Palace fashion. These wall paintings were probably the source for many embroidered textiles that depict landscapes (figs. 12, 21, and 27).

The Ottoman social structure was such that the dissemination of designs from the top of society is not surprising. The Ottoman court, as was the case with earlier Islamic empires, was the source of all knowledge and a place where ideas converged. The court moved with the capital over the centuries, from Bursa to Edirne and finally to İstanbul. These cities served as centers for skilled artists and craftsmen to employ their arts and crafts. After 1453, Topkapı Palace in İstanbul became a beacon drawing the most skilled artists, who benefited from royal patronage. The sultans were especially eager to welcome artists, hoping the association would assist their political rise; they wanted to be considered patrons and benefactors of the arts. Desiring to congregate in one place, artists from different ethnic and religious backgrounds and with different traditions and languages converged on the Ottoman capital, bringing with them many styles and new ideas. When European art began to penetrate Ottoman lands in the eighteenth century, skilled artists and artisans observed this new wave and created

Figure 26
Tombstone, Muradiye
Külliyesi, Bursa

Figure 27
Wall painting, Court of
concubines, Topkapı
Palace Harem, İstanbul

the unique style later called Turkish (Ottoman) Rococo. One result of these influences was a new style of Ottoman art, which melded traditional forms and shapes with the new, and was incorporated into Islamic ideology. This new imperial Ottoman style illustrated a desire to unite many ethnic groups speaking different languages and practicing different religions into one imperial Ottoman aesthetic, to establish and support its supremacy.

THE FUNCTIONS OF TEXTILES IN THE OTTOMAN HOME AND DAILY LIFE

Ottoman social life, though it was closed to many foreign observers, was very lively. Both within daily life and during celebrations, embroidered textiles held special significance. In order to understand the various functions of embroidered textiles, one must understand both the social environment and the occasions for which these textiles were produced and used.

An Ottoman house was generally a large single dwelling for an extended family and servants. It was situated at the side of its plot, flanked by a narrow cobbled

street on one side and by a garden on the other three. Built of wood, it was often two to three stories high. Most houses had a projecting upper storey where the main rooms were located, to catch some breeze on hot summer days or to provide a view. For privacy, the street side of the house contained fewer windows. The windows were covered with wooden lattices to prevent outside eyes from catching glimpses inside while allowing full air circulation. The other side of the house had a more open façade, with windows and balconies opening onto a garden filled with sweet-smelling flowers, mulberry, acacia, oriental plane and cypress trees, and singing birds, sometimes accompanied by small vegetable gardens and complemented with a fountain. The interior plan of the house was simple. The lower floor contained the kitchen, servant quarters, storage rooms, and the like. The second floor was reached by stairs that opened onto a medium-sized room, or an anteroom, or a large-sized hall. At least two other very large rooms opened onto this central hall. One of the large rooms was the *haremlik* (women's quarters) and the other, the *selamlık* (men's quarters). Other smaller rooms opened onto these

Figure 28
Interior view, Topkapı Palace Harem

Figure 29
Interior, engraving from Tableau general de l'Empire othoman *by Ignatius Mouradgea d'Ohsson (1740–1807), Imprimerie de monsieur (Firmin Didot) Paris, 1788–1824*

larger rooms or onto the entrance hall. Depending on the wealth of the owner, both the sizes of the rooms and their number increased. The main rooms of both the *haremlik* and *selamlık* were surrounded on three sides by *divan*s raised about a foot from the ground (fig. 1). Behind these were windows, opening onto the gardens or onto scenery outside. Cushions rested against the wall or were scattered at intervals along the *divan*s and were gaily embroidered with gold and colored silk threads, creating another garden inside the house. There were shelves, generally of wood or inlaid wood fitted into niches, placed along the fourth wall or flanking the *divan*s (fig. 28). On these shelves were placed objects, both those useful in daily life and ornamental. If the owner was wealthy enough to afford a summer and a winter room, the summer room contained a small fountain and winter room had a fireplace. Fireplaces were centrally located in a large room; they were usually decorated with ceramic tiles and covered with richly embroidered textiles such as large covers (cat. no. 40). The tandor was the primary heating equipment for cold, harsh, winter days. A small table with four short legs, it had a shelf of tin a few inches from the floor to hold a pan of charcoal enclosed in a metal screen. Over this table one or two large and thick wadded quilts were thrown, and members of the house-hold sat around with the quilts drawn over their knees (fig. 5). An Irish man, Buck Whaley, who visited the Ottoman Empire in the 1780s, mentioned such a tandor in his memoirs:

In Turkey none of the rooms have fire-places. The tendour is used in their stead. It is a square table with several quilted coverings spread over it, which reach down to the ground. Underneath the table is a large copper in which [charcoal?] *or embers are placed; the knees of each person round the table are covered with the quilted counterpane, and the head confined under the tendour, renders this place the most comfortable and of course the most frequented spot in the apartment. Round this, little parties are always assembled, either to read, work or for other amusements.*[13]

An Ottoman house was generally empty of any other standing furniture. This allowed each room to serve multiple functions – living room, dining room, or bedroom – at different times of day and night. For each activity, a set of equipment or collapsible furniture was brought out from the cupboards into the room as needed. This traditional interior set-up remained in use for a long time. It was observed by foreign visitors as late as toward the end of the nineteenth century.[14]

Meanwhile, among the newly rich, European-educated Ottomans of the nine-teenth century, European furniture became a symbol of status. Large tables with many chairs, four-poster beds with matching wardrobes and dressers, large couches, and free-standing cupboards began to appear in Ottoman houses. This new set of furniture was not portable; it necessitated specific rooms for specific functions. House plans started changing. Additional rooms for dining, sleeping, and living were added to the traditional plan. Except in the homes of very Europeanized families of İstanbul society, one important aspect remained the same until the end of the Ottoman Empire in 1924, and that was the division of the house into *haremlik* and *selamlık*.

Ottoman domestic life was divided into two parts, corresponding to the Ottoman house: the *haremlik* included the women's world as well as the men's private world, while the *selamlık* served as the men's public world. The walls of *haremlik* rooms were decorated with many textiles for festive occasions. The *selamlık* contained the rooms used by the male members of the family for the transaction of business, for formal receptions, and for the exercise of general hospitality involving male members of society. The *haremlik* part of the house was generally larger and contained the private apartments of the family. This was also where the women and children of the family lived from day to day and gathered

13 Whaley 1906, p. 72
14 Garnett 1917, pp. 220–24; Pardoe 1837,
      vol. 1, pp. 17–18

together with their male family members in the evenings. Women lived and worked in the *haremlik*. Here, they welcomed their female visitors, serving coffee and sweets on trays covered with richly embroidered textiles. This was also the place where many life-cycle ceremonies took place (fig. 29).

In any given home the day started early. After everyone got up, the bedding was gathered and rolled, to be put away in large wall cupboards. The bedding consisted of mattresses, quilts, and pillows spread on the divans at night or laid out on the carpeted floor of each room. Leyla Saz was the companion of one of the daughters of Sultan Abdülmecid in the second half of the nineteenth century. She mentions in her memoirs a similar practice in the *haremlik* of the Palace:

Real beds, or fixed beds, were rarely employed in those days. … The bed clothes were all quilted and were made from fine silk stuff, supple and light, covered in turn by silk material of a clear or embroidered design, sometimes with cashmere shawls as well. The Turkish coverlet is simply placed on top. It is a little wider and a little longer than the mattress itself. The cloth or lining of the coverlet is embroidered and lightly pulled back and tucked up on itself on all four sides; it was sewn with large stitches to the coverlet. The mattress and all the bedclothes were collected every morning, placed in a cupboard and kept there until the next evening. There were large pieces of cloth in square patterns, which were used to contain the bedclothes.[15]

What Leyla Saz described as the embroidered cloth incorporated into the coverlet might have been a later example of the large rectangular covers that date from the early seventeenth and eighteenth centuries (cat. nos. 3–16).[16] These large covers might have been used as wall hangings, either to decorate an empty wall, or to cover an already existing niche in the wall that was filled with objects required for daily use (fig. 30).[17] The close resemblance to wall tiles of the designs and design layouts of these covers might be another indication of their use as wall hangings (fig. 23). These covers seem to disappear from Ottoman homes sometime in the second half of the eighteenth century. While their use is still debated by scholars, these large covers illustrate the skilled workmanship of Ottoman embroidered textiles.

Another item Leyla Saz mentions in her memoirs is "large pieces of cloth in square patterns" known as *bohça*s. The *bohça* might be the oldest and longest-lived textile type used by the Turks. The first *bohça*s likely functioned as carrying cloths in a nomadic environment. Their use continued uninterrupted over many centuries and continues in Turkey today. A *bohça* is basically a square cloth which comes in many sizes (cat. nos. 20–22). It is used to wrap things to be carried or stored:

15 Saz 1994, p. 32
16 Taylor 1993, pp. 83–92; Taylor 1990, pp. 118–25
17 Erber 1995, p. 70; Denny 1981, p. 133; Johnstone 1985, p. 9. A painting by Osman Hamdi Bey dating to the second half of the nineteenth century in a private collection in İstanbul depicts such a cover hanging above a seated woman (Graham-Brown 1988, fig. 10).

Early in the morning, the stately Fatma Hanoum presented to my companion and myself a bokshalik *from the venerable Effendi, which consisted of the material for a dress, neatly folded in a handkerchief of clear muslin, fringed with gold-coloured silk.*[18]

The use of the *bohça* continued even after the introduction of dressers, indicating its importance as an object for the Ottomans. The old tradition of protecting your belongings by wrapping them with a textile remained strong:
Clothes and lingerie were placed in armoires, carefully wrapped up in two bohças, one on top of the other. A bohça, a square piece of material, sometimes large, sometimes small, sometimes richly ornamented and sometimes plain, was used to wrap up underwear, clothing and other articles of this nature in order to protect them from dust.[19]

Embroiderers took special care to prepare the *bohças* that were destined to be in a trousseau. Wedding *bohça*s protected the bride's trousseau during its transfer to her new house. They also exhibited the wealth of the bride and her family and her skill as an embroiderer (cat. no. 22). The *bohça* was one of the rare items that would be also viewed by the outsiders frequently in daily life. It was used to wrap ladies' dresses and towels while they were carried to the *hamam* (bathhouse) (fig. 31):
A complete outfit of fine garments for each lady is carried to the hammam by a

Figure 30
Harem, *Codex Vindobonensis (dated ca. 1590) Cod. 8626, fol. 116r. Osterreichische Nationalbibliothek, Vienna*

18 Pardoe 1837, pp. 121–22
19 Saz 1994, p. 325

*slave, tied up in a bokcha, or bundle-wrap – the primitive and universal portmanteau
– made generally of brocaded silk, and often embroidered with pearls and gold
thread . . . Other slaves carry rugs, towels, brass basins, and a score of other mys-
terious articles considered necessary for this important function, besides fruits and
refreshments.*[20]

Figure 31
On the Way to Hamam,
*German Archaeological
Institute, Istanbul*

Going to the *hamam* was a frequent outing for otherwise secluded Ottoman
women. It was both a festive and a ceremonial occasion.[21] Women sometimes
arrived at the *hamam* early in the morning. They might spend the entire day there
with neighbors and friends, chatting and catching up on the latest gossip, singing,
eating, and drinking, all the while washing themselves and their children. Besides
being a setting for the women's social gatherings, the *hamam* was an arena for
women and young girls to exhibit their exquisitely embroidered *bohça*s, bath towels,
dresses, and their bath *nalin*s (raised wooden clogs) and jewelry. It was rumored

20 Garnett 1904, p. 65; Garnett 1917, pp. 246–47
21 And 1994, pp. 242–51

that some ladies might have carried more than one or two sets of towels to change during the day and the best of their clothes just to show off their skill in embroidery and their family's wealth (cat. nos. 45–46). The *hamam* was also the place where mothers picked future brides for their sons; thus it was important for a young girl to present her skill in embroidery and her family's wealth and status, through these textiles, to prospective future mothers-in-law or matchmakers. If the desired match occurred, the bride's first *hamam* visit, which took place a few days after the wedding, was a ceremonial event. The first outing of a woman after giving birth was also to the *hamam*. Bath towels embroidered with colorful floral motifs on the narrow edges held an undiminished importance for every household.

Besides the exquisitely embroidered end panels of Turkish towels, the special weave of the ground fabric, which absorbed water quickly, was a surprise to many Europeans. Pietro Della Vella, who visited the Ottoman lands around 1614, wrote: *Nor must I omit mentioning a certain kind of cloth produced here (and made best of all in Salonika, where I have already arranged to be well furnished with it) which, as woven, has a pile on one side, namely the part of the lining; with the long, thick nap on the fabric just like our velvets; and from this sort of cloth they make various kinds of towels, large and small, and certain other items, not shirts but rather like jackets open in front, with loose sleeves, to put on over the naked skin when one comes out of the bath; for with this pile, when it is inside next to the skin, these garments dry one at once quickly and well all over. This is truly marvelous after bathing, either swimming or in the hot bath, and for women when they wash their hair, and deserves to be imitated in our country, though how I do not know.*[22]

Ottoman women's love of the bath and washing rituals astonished many Europeans and prompted Lady Elizabeth Craven, who lived in İstanbul in 1786, to write to her friend:
The Turkish women pass most of their time in the bath or upon their dress; strange pastime! The first spoils their person the last disfigures them. The frequent use of hot-baths destroys the folids, and these women at nineteen look older than I am at this moment. They endeavour to repair by art the mischief their constant soaking does to their charms; but till some one, more wise than the rest, finds out the cause of the premature decay of that invaluable gift, beauty, and sets an example to the rising generation of a different mode of life, they will always fade as fast as the roses they are so justly fond of.[23]

Women's lives were definitely not as lavishly 'spent' as Lady Craven suggested. Women were responsible for running large households with many children, slaves, and relatives. Many women were also involved in business, managing

Figure 32
Selamlık, *Topkapı Palace Library, İstanbul*

22 Della Valle 1990, p. 15
23 Craven 1970, p. 296

properties, or operating workshops from their homes through intermediaries.[24] In these large households there was always lots of activity. If it was not a day for the *hamam* or for a picnic to one of the many groves and creeks around İstanbul, it was a day for cleaning. A clean and well-kept house was a manifestation of how well a lady was raised. As well as cleaning and dusting, special care was taken to protect objects from dust by wrapping them in textiles. One of the cloths used for this purpose was the *kavuk* or *sarık*, used to cover a turban (cat. nos. 17–19). Until replaced by the *fez* in the nineteenth century, government officials wore *kavuk*s in many shapes and sizes to indicate their status in the government hierarchy. *Sarıkçılar* in *Kapalı çarşı* was the center of production for these elaborate turbans, which required specially trained personnel to assemble. A *kavuk* was made by sewing many layers of stuffed cloth and attaching them to one another. Once sewn, a *kavuk* was never dismantled. It was kept on a special stand at home called a *kavukluk*. To protect it from gathering dust when not in use, a textile specially made for that purpose was placed over it. These covers were square in shape with a circle set in the center of the square.[25] A painting in the Topkapı Palace Museum's Library shows a royal procession with the sultan riding on his horse; his palace attendant, who took care of his turbans, is shown walking beside him, carrying his secondary turban wrapped in what appears to be an embroidered textile (fig. 32).

Another textile that expressed the Ottoman fascination with covering and wrapping was a small rectangular cover of a loom-width fabric of about 50 cm width and 140–150 cm length (cat. nos. 27–29). The whole surface was covered with embroidery, incorporating motifs that were used elsewhere in other embroidered textiles. These motifs repeated in the same direction many times on the surface of the fabric; in some examples, the direction of the motifs was flipped (cat. no. 29). These covers are referred to as mirror covers in many publications. They are described as hanging over mirrors to ward off the evil eye.[26] The small size of mirror covers might have allowed them to be used in other circumstances as well, for example as covers for serving trays, or covers for babies sleeping in their carved wooden cradles, or for *Kur'an*s placed on shelves or reading stands called *rahle*s. Julia Pardoe mentions such a stand in her memoirs: *Along a silken cord, on either side of the niche, were hung a number of napkins, richly worked and fringed with gold; and a large copy of the Koran was deposited beneath a handkerchief of gold gauze, on a carved rosewood bracket.*[27]

Visitors always enlivened the secluded lives of Ottoman women. They were welcomed with joy both for the fresh change they brought to the lives of the

24 Gerber 1980, pp. 231–44
25 Taylor 1993, pp. 93–97
26 *Ibid.*, pp. 99–103
27 Pardoe 1837, p. 18

household inhabitants, and for the age-old tradition instilled in the people that a guest was a 'guest from God.' Thus, every whim of a guest had to be indulged in a gracious manner. Over the centuries, visitations evolved into elaborate ceremonies. While the hostess was honoring her guests, she also made sure she showed off her skills in running her household, cooking, and embroidering. Right after guests arrived at the house, they were shown into the best room of the *haremlik*. It was the lady of the house who inquired after the health of her guests, and their husbands and children, at length. After several courtesies were exchanged in the reception rooms, sweets and coffee were brought in one after another on trays covered with embroidered textiles. Guests were presented with embroidered napkins or towels to wipe their hands before and after they tasted a variety of sweets presented in crystal or gold cups encrusted with gems (cat. nos. 30–39):

But the most beautiful objects employed during the repast were the silver basin, strainer, and a vase, that were held by two black slaves for us to wash our hands, while a third stood a pace behind them, bearing upon her arm the napkin, wrought with a border of flowers in coloured silks, whereon they were to be dried.[28]

While we were indulging ourselves with that refreshing beverage, light, beautifully cut-glass cups with covers, similar to those used in Europe for custards, only having two handles to them, placed in small saucers filled with different kinds of sherbet, were passed round on frosted silver trays of exquisite workmanship, over which were negligently thrown embroidered rose-pink silk napkins, which the slaves removed as they drew near to us. … This refreshment being over, the Circassian slaves then knelt down and presented each of us with a gold salver, on which was placed a fine embroidered muslin napkin, fringed with a deep border of gold lace, with which we just touched our lips according to the custom of the country.[29]

In the nineteenth century, European women who were visiting the Ottoman lands often found ways to be invited to Ottoman homes to indulge their curiosity. Like Caroline Paine, who visited the wife of the Governor of Bursa, some of these ladies took lessons ahead of time, learning how to act in such gatherings:

Directly after we were seated we were offered sweetmeats, served upon a superb waiter of silver and gold; a small, beautiful basket of gold contained spoons of the same, and an empty one, the fellow to it, was to receive the spoons after they had been used. We had learned previously, while in Pera, the manner of taking sweetmeats when offered in the East, namely, to take one tea-spoonful from the dish, and place the spoon, after using it, in the empty cup always brought for that purpose. So we were prepared, happily, to go through the ceremony without making any dis-

28 Pardoe 1837, pp. 216–54
29 Lott 1866, pp. 220–21

اشنی قالمش یکی سونمش فیل | تللی صاحبن قیلدی اوطرف خلیل

هرشکنن طولوسفیداج ایدر | افلعله صفحهٔ برعلاج ایدر

دخلراولوراکیکی برکٔزر | کهنه بهاری وفنی ولوب یکیٔزر

برجکه سی بغلواولویه دونز | جنبر ایله چهرهٔ بی نوروم ز

ای باشنی اورتلو صارترهمان | ال دودق عیبنی ایرنهان

وهمله اوقور برکیکی قل اعوذ | برده سنی قالدرجی دیرنعوذ

حقدن اندٔ فرقتٔ ایدی نیاز | حاجت اجون صکره کرقیکه نماز

حرصی بود که اوایکن ول بی نوا | ابوعیب و فریتونه زنه مبتلا

برده عجوزی کجی هریری سرد | مرکه مراد ایدک و درد دینه در

قصه سی جون کوز که غسال ایدک | قارنی ایسه قبهٔ انجال ایدی

قاره قوری رقاوردق درشت ایدک | سوزلری اتش دینی انکشت ایدک

Figure 33
Casanova Marrying an
Old Woman, *from
Hamse-i Ata-i (1728),
inv. no. R816, y102a
(Karatay T.2392),
Topkapı Palace Library,
İstanbul*

Figure 34
European Diplomat
Being Received by
Grand Vizier's
Kaymakam, *watercolor
by an anonymous Greek
artist,* ca. 1809–10, *inv.
no. D.124–1895, Victoria
and Albert Museum,
London*

creditable blunder. The conserve was followed by coffee, brought in a small silver kettle, suspended by three chains, while another slave bore exquisite little cups of gold upon a tray of gold and silver. A third filled the cups, and a fourth, taking the foot of the cup between the thumb and first finger, presented it to the guest. A fifth completed the ceremony, by bringing a muslin napkin, embroidered in gold and colors. When the cup was returned, the servant made use of both hands, placing the left beneath and the right above at the same instant.[30]

If the guests were invited to dine with the hostess, the necessary articles were brought in by servants, slaves, and young girls of the household who set up the reception room for dining.[31] First a round cover was spread on the floor. This spread alone sometimes served as a table; at other times a cylindrical stand was put on top of it (fig. 33 and cat. nos. 1–2). The lavish food tray was brought and set on top. Guests were welcomed and offered water to wash their hands and *yağlık*s to wipe them. Everyone sat cross-legged around the table placing their embroidered *yağlık*s on their laps to protect themselves from spills (fig. 34 and cat. nos. 30–39).

This type of table setup was also in use in the sultan's palace. Mary Nisbet, Lady Elgin described such a table in her letters, which was set for four British men who

30 Paine 1859, p. 54
31 And 1994, pp. 176–81

were installing a chandelier in the Palace in the late eighteenth century:
They were treated with dinner on a silver gilt table with a beautiful embroidered cloth laid under it, and embroidered napkins.[32]

In the nineteenth century, there were Ottoman households that continued to serve dinners in the old fashion:

Covers are laid on sofras [a tray stand] *– circular tables, or rather stands, raised only some eight inches from the floor, and accommodating at the most half a dozen*

persons. Turkish tables consist merely of a spoon and portion of bread. Round the raised leather pad, which occupies the centre, are grouped small saucers containing hors-d'oeuvres – olives, cubes of watermelon or cucumber, radishes, anchovies, etc. As the ladies seat themselves cross-legged on the low cushions disposed around the sofra, slaves approach bearing water, soap, and embroidered towels. Other towels with ends embroidered in coloured silks and gold thread – the chevreh of which the East has of late years been almost emptied by the demand for them in the West – are distributed as table napkins, and the repast commences.[33]

32　Ferguson 1926, p. 54
33　Garnett 1909, p. 274

Figure 35
Girl Carrying a Coffee Tray, *by Ruben Seroupyan, Demirbank, İstanbul*

Figure 36
Bride and Her Trousseau, *drawn between 1645–50, inv. no. 2380, y.112, Deniz Müzesi Kitaplığı, İstanbul*

There were also families who served food 'the old way' to please their guests. In her memoirs, Emine Foat Tugay, a Turkish lady born in 1897, described a luncheon arranged in the "old Turkish style" in 1908:

A few days later, Mme. Tinayre came to a ladies' luncheon, arranged in the old Turkish style at our house. A very large round cloth of purple watered silk, heavily embroidered and fringed with gold thread, was spread on the floor of the dining room, from which the table had previously been removed. A stool, placed in its cen-

ter and covered by a smaller copy of the cloth, served to support a circular silver tray, which was large enough to allow six persons to sit comfortably around it on six stiff brocade cushions. Turkish food, served in the traditional round dishes with covers, was placed in the middle of the tray, each person helping herself in turn. There was no cloth on the tray.[34]

After dinner, coffee was served. In Ottoman times, as in traditional Turkey today, if a visitor were served a cup of coffee, that visitor would remember and pray for the kindness of the host for forty years to come. The service of such an

34 Tugay 1963, pp. 266–67

important beverage was very ceremonious and conducted by at least two or three young girls or boys. Depending up on the wealth of the host, the instruments, cups, and embroidered cloths used for this occasion could be very sumptuous (fig. 35 and cat. no. 41). Leyla Saz described in her memoirs such a service to Sultan Abdülaziz in the Çirağan Palace in the late nineteenth century:

The coffee arrived fully prepared in a coffeepot made of gold and was placed on hot cinders which were in a sort of a golden basin, suspended at the end of three chains held high by a servant. This disposition was known as a sitil *or a small brazier. Two of the servants held a gold tray on which were small coffee cups in fine porcelain from Saxony or from China along with saucers in finely inlaid gold embellished with small, precious stones. At the same time, these two girls held a cloth of silk or of velvet, richly embroidered with gold, pearls, small precious stones and with a central motif in diamonds, all surrounded by a fringe of gold. It was folded diagonally and the girls each held one end in the palm of their hands at the same time as they held the tray in such a way that the edge of the tray was covered by the cloth which fell down on both sides. The first mistress of the coffee service would take a saucer from the tray and carefully place a coffee cup on it; then with a small quilted piece of linen, which was always on the tray, she took the handle of the coffeepot and poured the coffee. She would then, with great delicacy, take the base of the saucer with the end of her fingers in such a fashion that it rested on the tip of her thumb and in this way she carried it to the Sultan with gesture full of grace and skill.*[35]

When the guests were ready to leave, the lady of the house presented them with gifts, generally in the form of embroidered textiles. Depending on the wealth of the host, these gifts ranged from a single embroidered *yağlık* to a set of clothing presented in an embroidered *bohça*. In Ottoman daily life any important letter, sum of money, present of jewelry, gift of fruit or sweets, or article of clothing was wrapped in an embroidered *yağlık* or *bohça*. The richer the wrapper, the greater the compliment. These textiles were so intermingled with daily life that even in sporting competitions such as archery the reward of victory was an embroidered *yağlık*.[36] In the 1830s, at the end of her visit to the *harem* of Reis Efendi (Minister for Foreign Affairs), Julia Pardoe received a generous gift from the lady of the house. Miss Pardoe conveys to us in her writings the importance of the gift to the giver and its intended meaning for the recipient:

We returned to the great centre saloon where the other ladies awaited us, surrounded by a crowd of slaves, one of whom carried upon a salver a pile of embroidered handkerchiefs, worked by the fair fingers of the two younger Hanoums, with gold thread and coloured silks. This gift, which had been prepared for me, was accompanied by

35 Saz 1994, pp. 49–50
36 de Busbecq 1968, p. 134

a thousand kindly comments. I was desired to examine one piece of needlework, and to remark that I carried away with me the heart of the donor. Upon another I was told that I should find a bouquet of flowers, and discover that they had presented me with the portrait which they should retain of me in their own memories.[37]

Festivities and ceremonies were as numerous as they were varied in Ottoman life. Feasts and festivities for *bayram*s (religious holidays), weddings, and circumcisions were occasions at which young and old, rich and poor came together. For every level of society, including the sultan, these events were occasions to celebrate, by providing everyone who knocked at your door with the best you could afford in food, clothing, gifts, and entertainment. Ottoman chronicles from the sixteenth century onwards were full of narration and illustrations documenting different festivities for circumcisions of royal sons, weddings of royal daughters, and celebrations welcoming newborns into the royal family. These royal festivities sometimes lasted for several months.[38] The rest of the populace also celebrated life-cycle ceremonies and religious holidays, although entertainment was not as lavishly organized as at the Palace. In the chronicles, Ottomans do not dwell on the role of women in royal ceremonies. But in ordinary homes, women were the organizers of many of these events with their menfolk. As was the custom, men and women celebrated events segregated from one another in different parts of the house. We know more about the gatherings organized by women. This is thanks to European women travelers of the nineteenth century who described these events vividly, and modern Turkish women who recalled their childhood memories of older traditions in the late nineteenth and the early twentieth centuries.

In Ottoman society, the most important event for a woman was her wedding.[39] Preparations for a marriage began early. From the time a girl was born, the elder women of her family started working on her *çeyiz* (trousseau). When a young girl reached an age to be able to hold a needle she joined the same effort. She devoted much of her time to embroidering *yağlık*s, bath towels, covers of different sizes, and other articles for her home, as well as *uçkur*s, *çevre*s, shirts, dresses, pants, and many other fashion accouterments for herself.

Families arranged marriages for their daughters and sons. The designated boy and girl had little say in the matter. In Ottoman society there was a distinct difference between the agreement of the marriage contract and the actual wedding. The marriage contract was a civil act establishing an economic relationship between a woman and a man and could take place long before the wedding. The

37 Pardoe 1837, p. 270

38 And 1994, pp. 157–67. Two of the well-known manuscripts that depict such events are *Surnama*, Topkapı Palace Museum H.1344 (circumcision ceremonies of Crown Prince Mehmet, son of Murat III in 1582) and *Surnama-i Vehbi*, Topkapı Palace Museum A.3593 (circumcision celebrations of the sons of Ahmet III in 1720).

39 Kayaoğlu 1998, pp. 20–37; Goodwin 1997, pp. 114–15; And 1994, pp. 211–21

Figure 37
The Day After the
Wedding, *Sevgi Gönül
Collection, İstanbul*

wedding, on the other hand, was a public announcement of the marriage between the two families and its communal celebration. After the long wedding festivities and the arrival of the bride in a celebratory procession to her new home, the couple began to live as husband and wife. Days before the bride was transferred to her new home, her relatives and friends proceeded to decorate her new home with the items in her trousseau, which were retrieved from finely embroidered wedding *bohça*s (cat. no. 22). While some of the pieces from the trousseau were spread with a view to artistic effect, some items like *yağlık*s and bath towels were hung from strings that were attached along the walls (fig. 36). After these preparations the bride arrived in her new home a couple of days later dressed in a magnificent dress and a veil. She wore shoes as elaborately embroidered as her dress (fig. 37 and cat. nos. 56 and 57).[40] Seated amid her trousseau, on which she had worked for so many years just for this occasion, the bride and her possessions were presented to the curious eyes of the guests, who would inspect her handiwork and judge her skills. Caroline Paine went to such a wedding and described the bride and her trousseau as follows:

... Her [the bride's] *dress was of scarlet cashmere, heavily and tastefully wrought with gold, the* antari *and trousers being of the same material. A closely-fitting fez, nearly concealed by wreaths of diamonds, in the forms of flowers and fruit, covered her head. From the left side projected ungracefully, two long ostrich feathers, one red, the other lilac, and a veil of silver lace two or three feet in length, fell on each side of her face. Her long, glossy black hair, plaited and curled at the ends, hung down her back. Her fingers were loaded with rings of precious stones, and in her lap was a red silk pockethandkerchief. Her face was beautiful, the complexion slightly brunette, with fine color, the eyes black, bright, and sparkling, and the splendor of the* tout ensemble *was heightened by the odd decoration of diamonds upon the face. Clusters of diamonds, in the form of a star, were placed, one upon the forehead, one upon the chin, and one upon each cheek. ...*

Leaving that room [where the bride was sitting] *we came to another which contained the trousseau of the bride. Here were the most costly dresses of rich silks and superb embroideries, magnificent cashmere shawls, gems, slippers, &c.*[41]

While eating, singing, dancing, and merriment were underway in the *haremlik*s of both the bride's and the groom's houses, the *selamlık*s would witness similar festivities. One of these festivities was the ceremonial shaving of the beard and cutting of the hair of the bridegroom on the day of the arrival of the bride to her new home. The bridegroom would be seated on a chair with a ceremonial apron and towel placed upon him (fig. 38 and cat. nos. 43 and 44). The barber would

40 See Micklewright MS for further discussion of changing styles and fashions in the Ottoman wedding dress in the late nineteenth century.

41 Paine 1859, pp. 62–64

start his work under the watchful eyes of the bridegroom's relatives and friends. All the while the musicians would be playing and singing cheerfully. Before the day's end, the bridegroom was obliged to pray for the good fortune bestowed on him and for the future of himself and his new family. He performed his prayers in front of his wife in the privacy of the newlyweds' bedroom, on a richly embroidered prayer cloth (cat. no. 42).

After the marriage, the next big festivity took place at the time of the birth of the first child; each successive newborn was welcomed with similar festivities. Childbearing and childrearing, more than marriage itself, transformed men and women into socially mature adults in Ottoman society, thus the society's insistence on celebrating this new step for the parents and welcoming the newborn as the cause of this change.[42] The day after the birth, one of the biggest rooms of the *haremlik* was decorated with the same textiles from the new mother's bridal trousseau as had also bedecked her nuptial chamber (fig. 39). The mother and child were dressed in their finest and were then laid on a sumptuous bed covered with the finest quilt the household could afford. In wealthy households these quilts were richly embroidered with gold and silver metallic threads, pearls, and gems. Once the mother and newborn were settled in their bed a long train of guests would arrive, dressed in their finest clothes and jewels and carrying symbolic gifts according to their resources. They were served with coffee, tea, or a special sherbet made with red-dyed sugar and cloves. Sipping one of these, the guests would call on God to bless the mother's milk and protect both the mother and newborn from evil spirits. Lucy Garnett described such a scene:

New mother's bed spread with elaborately embroidered and fringed sheets of native gauze and covered with quilts of satin crusted with needlework in gold and silver thread. At the head are piled half a dozen long narrow silken pillows enclosed in 'slips' matching the sheets. Around the lady's head is bound a crimson kerchief to which is attached a bunch of charms, a gauze veil of the same hue being thrown loosely over them – the whole coiffure designed to keep the peris at a distance. ... New born is at once tightly swathed in cotton bandages under a libarde, or gown of quilted cotton stuff. Various quilted wrappers bound one over another. Head is covered with a little cap of red silk from which hangs a tassel of seed pearls and a bunch of amulets. The baby lay on a quilt in the cradle, and over it is spread a large square of crimson gauze.[43]

The mother's textiles and accessories would similarly be used to decorate the bed on which her little boy would lie during his circumcision ceremony. Generally groups of boys who were the same age from the same neighborhood were

42 Pierce 1997, pp. 169–96
43 Garnett 1909, pp. 227–28

circumcised together. The cost of the festivities was covered by the wealthiest parents. Thus the circumcision ceremonies were also neighborhood events that brought many people together. Before the event, the boys were all dressed with new clothing and caps decorated with charms. After the operation they were laid on beds richly decorated with textiles embroidered by their mothers and grandmothers.

Ottoman costume was one of the key areas of decorative arts representing Ottoman culture. The imperial Ottoman costume was worn throughout the empire by the ruling élite, and was imitated in the provincial towns by the populace. It was the fashionable attire of the day and through dressing in this style, individuals sought to achieve status, influence, and wealth. The history of costume in Ottoman lands presents a complex and varied evolution. Both men and women's costumes changed gradually over the centuries, but certain items retained their overall shape and functions, although losing and gaining minor characteristic features.

Ottomans were always careful of their attire. They attached the greatest importance and value to clothes, because in the traditionally structured Ottoman society, what one wore indicated one's religion, rank, and class. Emelia Hornby, who stayed in İstanbul in the mid-nineteenth century, draws us a vivid image of the dresses worn by women at the time:

Her [Rıza Paşa's first wife] *selma, or wide-sleeved under-dress, (trousers, etc.) was of a delicate violet-color, bound round the waist by a richly embroidered scarf; her shirt of silvery Broussa gauze. Over this was a magnificent jacket of amber-colored cashmere, lined with the richest sable. On her head she wore a fez, bound round with a large plait of hair, which was fastened every here and there with immense rose-diamonds. A purple lily-flower was stuck straight down this plait, and shaded her forehead.*[44]

Her [Rıza Paşa's second wife] *trousers, and the robe which twists round the feet, and trails behind, were of the most brilliant blue, edged with a little embroidery of white. Her cashmere jacket was of pale lilac (like double primroses), lined with gold-colored fur. Delicate lilac gauze handkerchief was twined round her head; among the fringes of which, diamond hearts-eases, of the natural size, glittered on golden stalks, which trembled at the slightest movement. Lilac slippers, embroidered with seed pearls, completed her toilette.*[45]

Men and women's costumes were similar until the nineteenth century. Both men and women wore *şalvar* (loose pants), a *gömlek* (shirt), and robes – *entari* for women and *kaftan* for men. Men wore a *kavuk* or a small turban when they went out. Women wore elaborate hairstyles, which changed frequently and included skull caps, large pillbox hats, scarves, needlepoint flowers, and jewelry.

44 Hornby 1858, p. 249
45 *Ibid.*, p. 251

Figure 38
Barber, *inv. no. 8:0, nr10,
19a, The Royal Library,
Stockholm*

Figure 39
The Nursery of a
Distinguished Turkish
Woman, *by J.B.
Vanmoor,* SK-A-2003,
*Rijkmuseum,
Amsterdam*

The *uçkur* and the *çevre* were two garment pieces used by the Ottomans. The *uçkur* was a sash, approximately 200 cm long and 30 cm wide, used both by men and women (cat. nos. 47–55). It was drawn through the wide seam of the *şalvar* and knotted in front to hold the baggy pants tight around the waist. Both ends of the *uçkur* were embroidered so that when tied, the ends dangled down the front as adornment (fig. 40).

A çevre was a square cloth approximately 90 × 90 cm in size embroidered along all four sides. It was most often used as a headscarf (fig. 41 and cat. nos. 23–26). It was placed either folded or unfolded on the head and fastened beneath the chin. Sometimes it was wrapped around a cap or combined with other headscarves and attached with pins or jewelry to the hair. Aside from being a fashion accouterment, the çevre was used as a packing or wrapping cloth like the bohça. In her book, Julia Pardoe mentions such a headscarf, worn by Reis Efendi's wife Devlehai Hanım:

Devlehai Hanoum was dressed in an entary of white silk, embroidered all over with groups of flowers in pale green; her salva, or trowsers, were of satin of the Stuart tartan, and her jacket light blue; the gauze that composed her chemisette was almost impalpable, and the cachemire about her waist was of a rich crimson. Her hair, of which several tresses had been allowed to escape from beneath the embroidered handkerchief, was as black as the plumage of a raven.[46]

The influence of European fashion, especially on women's costume, intensified in the nineteenth century. After laws were passed to make 'modern' clothing compulsory for both men and women, European-style garments were accepted: pants and coat for men and long dresses for women.[47] Initially, small features were added to traditional costume. Lace collars and cuffs, for example, embellished the *gömlek*. Eventually more or less entirely European-style costumes appeared.

Figure 40
Palace Maiden, *by Levni, 1732, Topkapı Palace Library, İstanbul*

Figure 41
Woman in Outdoor Costume, *by Levni, 1732, Topkapı Palace Library, İstanbul*

The best example of this transformation of women's costume was the *bindallı*, a type of dress for special occasions such as weddings, worn both by the bride, and her family and friends (cat. no. 56). Its distinguishing characteristics are the floral designs and *dival* embroidery applied on the ground fabric.

The *bindallı* appears to have been introduced to Ottoman women's fashion along with dresses and skirts from Europe. Although there are a few examples assembled with baggy pants, most of the *bindallı*s were long dresses, sometimes

46 Pardoe 1837, pp. 214–15
47 See Scarce 1987; And 1994; Micklewright MS; Micklewright 1989; and Micklewright 1990 for further discussion of the changing lifestyles and fashions of the Ottoman Empire.

with matching fitted jackets and slippers (cat. no. 57). They exhibited many variations, especially in their tailoring, through the nineteenth and early twentieth centuries.[48]

Ottoman costume and embroidered textiles for domestic use are wonderful sources through which to explore changes in Ottoman society. Embroidery was an art form produced by a large part of the population, both commercially and domestically. Finished products were so much a part of Ottoman daily life that they were inseparable from it. Thus they offer a unique window onto urban society in the Ottoman Empire. The drastic changes taking place in Ottoman society and culture between the sixteenth and the twentieth centuries are very clearly reflected in the embroidered textiles of the period. They become tools with which to explore the changing social and economic aspects of Ottoman culture.

48 See Mickelwright MS and And 1994 for
   further discussion on the *bindallı*

Glossary

ATMA STITCH

A type of flat stitch, this stitch is actually a combination of two stitches: a single-faced satin stitch and Bukharan couching.

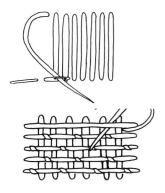

Sometimes known as the Oriental stitch, it is worked in two steps (de Dillmont 1978, p. 166). A single-faced satin stitch is used to cover the whole motif area, using unspun silk. Then a plied silk thread is laid over the first layer of embroidered unspun silk threads at a ninety-degree angle. This second layer of plied silk thread is secured by bringing the same plied silk thread up from below.

BUKHARAN STITCH

A type of self-couching stitch in which the couching thread secures down the previously laid stitch with small slanting stitches on the jour-

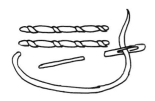

ney back. Both the couching thread and couched thread are the same. In appearance, the couching stitch is short on the front face and long on the back face of the fabric (Thomas 1954, p. 55).

CHAIN STITCH

One of the looped stitches worked with either a needle or a hook. If worked with a needle, the thread is brought up at the beginning of the row. The needle is then inserted into the same hole where the thread first emerged, forming a loop, and is brought up through the fabric again a short distance beyond. It is then brought out through and over the loop of working thread. If the stitch is done with a hook, the thread is hooked from above and pulled through to create a loop. This loop is then secured with another loop pulled through the same way (Thomas 1954, pp. 32–33).

COUCHING

In this technique, the embroidery threads are laid on the surface of the fabric and secured with small stitches, using a second thread (Thomas 1954, p. 55).

COMPOSITE STITCHES

A structure made up of two or more component stitches, each of which can be analyzed separately. *Atma* and whipped stitches are examples of composite stitches (The Lloyd Cotsen Textile Documentation Project, The Textile Museum 1998).

COUNTED WORK

General term for embroidery worked and disposed by counting horizontal and/or vertical warp and weft yarns; may be worked with flat, crossed, looped, or composite stitches (The Lloyd Cotsen Textile Documentation Project, The Textile Museum 1998).

CROSSED STITCHES

A unit stitch composed of two flat stitches crossing the same small area at opposite or oblique angles. Each flat stitch may be crossed before the next is worked, or a whole row of parallel slanting stitches may be worked first, and the crossing stitches worked in a second 'journey.' Crossed stitches may be counted or not. Fishbone, herringbone, and Rhodian cross stitches are a few examples of this category (The Lloyd Cotsen Textile Documentation Project, The Textile Museum 1998).

DIVAL EMBROIDERY

An embroidery style sometimes referred to as *maraş işi*, from the town of Maraş in southeastern Turkey. A paper cutout design is pasted over the ground fabric using special glue. The embroidery is then worked by holding a group of gold metallic-wrapped threads and moving them from side to side on top of the fabric over the paper cutout design. During this process, on each side, the metal threads are then secured to the ground fabric with a separate couching thread (Yüksel 1997, pp. 356–76).

DOUBLE RUNNING STITCH

A type of flat stitch, this stitch consists of a simple running stitch worked in two journeys over the same line. This stitch, which appears the same on both sides, is

known by several names: Holbein stitch, line, square, stroke, two-sided line, two-sided stroke, and Romanian stitch (Thomas 1954, pp. 121–22).

EYELET STITCH

A type of flat stitch, this stitch consists of a series of back stitches worked in pairs, disposed from the same center (The Lloyd Cotsen Textile Documentation Project, The Textile Museum 1998).

FISHBONE STITCH

A type of crossed stitch, generally worked as a filling stitch. A series of slanted crossed stitches, with satin stitches taken alternately from one side to the other and crossing at the center of the work, near the base of

Uçkur (sash), late 18th or early 19th century. Detail from The Textile Museum 1.88 (cat. no. 50)

each individual stitch (The Lloyd Cotsen Textile Documentation Project, The Textile Museum 1998).

FLAT STITCHES

Stitches formed by working the needle alternately in and out of a fabric and thus laying the sewing element flat and straight on first one face and then, depending on the stitch, making a return journey along the same line. Running, double running, satin, stem, back, and outline stitches are a few of the stitches in this category. Stitches may be parallel to the axis of the fabric weave, oblique or diagonal. They may be equal or unequal in length on either face. Distinctions may be made between stitches derived from the running stitch, which progress from entry point to entry point, and stitches derived from the back stitch, which have a regressive (or wrapping) motion between entry points. This distinction does not always reflect reversibility. Flat stitches may be worked singly, along a line, in vertical or horizontal rows, and disposed in a straight or slanted manner on the surface (The Lloyd Cotsen Textile Documentation Project, The Textile Museum 1998).

HERRINGBONE STITCH

A type of crossed stitch worked in a row with both arms occurring equal length, evenly spaced. The crossed points of the stitches touch each other at top and bottom. It pro-

duces horizontal parallel lines of single straight stitches in alternating alignment on the reverse (The Lloyd Cotsen Textile Documentation Project, The Textile Museum 1998).

KASNAK ISI
See tambour work.

KNOTTED STITCHES

A looped structure in which the loop(s) are secured by a flat stitch to form a knot. Bullion, Peking knot, and pearl stitch are examples of knotted stitches (The Lloyd Cotsen Textile Documentation Project, The Textile Museum 1998, Emery 1994, p. 244).

LOOPED STITCHES

Stitches in which the element is made to deviate from a direct line and held out of line by the next stitch; the process can be described as looping the thread under the needle. Chain, buttonhole, feather, and cable stitch are a few of the stitches in this category (The Lloyd Cotsen Textile Documentation Project, The Textile Museum 1998; Emery 1994, pp. 241–43).

MUSABAK STITCH

A type of composite stitch utilizing single faggot and reversed faggot stitches. The faggot stitch is a counted stitch worked on the diagonal. It is made up of a series of straight flat stitches on the surface, producing a square; generally worked in rows as

a filling or in pulled thread work. It produces parallel diagonal rows of straight stitches on the reverse (The Lloyd Cotsen Textile Documentation Project, The Textile Museum 1998;

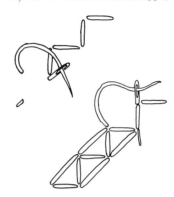

Ellis 1989, pp. 138–40). In the *Muṣabak* stitch a single faggot stich is generally worked on the first journey and then a reversed faggot stitch on the journey back.

M RVER STITCH

A type of flat stitch worked as a counted stitch and used in openwork embroidery. How this stitch was worked is not clear. A possible explanation is given by Marianne Ellis in her 1989 article in *Embroidery* magazine (Ellis 1989, pp. 138–40).

OPENWORK

An embroidery style identified by holes or spaces in or between elements of a fabric either as an integral part of the structure or as a result of accessory stitching. It is produced by a variety of textile-working techniques.

PATTERN DARNING

A method of disposing running stitches as a filling to create one or more patterns. It is usually worked by counting warp and weft yarns of the ground fabric (The Lloyd Cotsen Textile Documentation Project, The Textile Museum 1998).

PULLED WORK

An embroidery technique characterized by warp and weft yarns of a ground fabric pulled out of alignment and held in place with embroidery stitches under tension; drawn-fabric work is a British term for pulled work. It is used for openwork-style embroidery and is sometimes termed 'deflected element work.'

ROMANIAN STITCH

A type of self-couching stitch in which the couching thread holds down the first long stitch with long loose slanting stitches on the journey back. Both the couching thread and couched thread are the same. In appearance, the couching stitch is

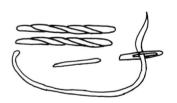

long on the front face and short on the back face of the fabric (Thomas 1954, p. 56).

RUNNING STITCH

A series of straight flat stitches worked along a line in a continual forward motion through the ground fabric; stitches may or may not be of equal length on the face and/or the reverse. Worked in a single line as an outline, or in rows to create a filling (Thomas 1954, p. 177).

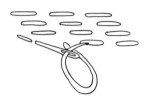

SATIN STITCH

A type of flat stitch in which simple straight flat stitches are disposed by laying a series of straight stitches parallel and close together on both faces of the ground cloth. Each stitch returns on the reverse of the cloth to a point contiguous to its starting point so that the area is covered on both faces by identical stitches (Thomas 1954, p. 179).

SELF-COUCHING

A couching technique in which the same yarn that is used to create the 'float' across the surface of the fabric is used on the return pass to tie down the long straight float with a short straight or a long slanting stitch.

SINGLE-FACED SATIN STITCH

A variation of the satin stitch which does not cover both faces of the

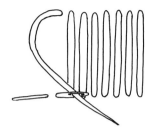

fabric with identical stitches. This stitch was often used to conserve thread, and is also called the surface satin stitch (Thomas 1954, p. 180).

STITCH

One complete movement of an element through a fabric or portion of a fabric structure by means of a needle or some equivalent implement; also, the portion of the element disposed in or on the fabric by such a movement (Emery 1994, p. 232). Simple stitch structures fall into five general categories: flat, looped, knotted, crossed, and composite (The Lloyd Cotsen Textile Documentation Project, The Textile Museum 1998).

TAMBOUR WORK

An embroidery technique known as *Kasnak işi* in Turkish. This technique is applied by working a chain stitch through the fabric with a pointed hook, also known as a tambour hook. The term tambour refers to the round hoop frame in which the ground fabric was secured (The Lloyd Cotsen Textile Documentation Project, The Textile Museum 1998).

TURKISH STITCH

A type of flat stitch, also known as the triangular two-sided stitch, worked by counting warp and weft yarns and diagonal to the ground fabric. The needle always passes over and under the same number of warp and weft yarns in a diagonal line. On the journey back the needle follows the same line and the threads forms slanting stitches (de Dillmont 1978, pp. 97–98).

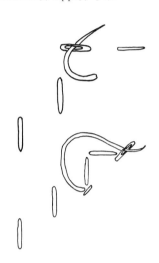

Z- OR S-SPUN

These terms refer to the direction(s) of a single yarn's twist. A yarn is Z-spun if, when held in a vertical position, the spiral conforms to the slant of the central portion of the letter 'Z' and S-spun if the spiral conforms to the slant of the central portion of the letter 'S' (Emery 1994, p. 11). The terms s2z or z2s refer to the direction(s) of two or more yarns twisted (plied) together. The first letter indicates the direction of the indi-

vidual yarn's spin, the number in the middle indicates how many yarns were twisted (plied) together, and the final letter indicates the direction of the ply.

1

Floor spread (left)
Late 17th or early 18th century
The Textile Museum 1.4
Acquired by George Hewitt
Myers in 1915
FOUNDATION
Warp: linen, Z-spun, 19/cm, blue
Weft: linen, Z-spun, 20/cm, blue
Structure: balanced plain weave
Dimensions: diameter 134.5 cm
Construction: four panels sewn
together; fully lined with dark-
red cotton fabric
EMBROIDERY
Embroidery thread: silk, z2s, six
colors: medium blue, dark red,
pink, yellow, white, light green
Embroidery stitch: 3/1 running
stitch in diagonal alignment
(warp and weft directions)
NOTES
Embroidered before assembly

2

Floor spread (right)
Late 17th or early 18th century
The Textile Museum 1.3
Acquired by George Hewitt
Myers in 1915
FOUNDATION
Warp: linen, Z-spun, 17/cm,
undyed
Weft: linen, Z-spun, 14/cm,
undyed
Structure: balanced plain weave
Dimensions: diameter 139.5 cm
Construction: two panels sewn
together
Edge finish: rolled and hemmed
EMBROIDERY
Embroidery threads:
Silk, unspun, five colors: red,
green, blue, light green, white
Silk, z2s, four colors: red, white,
blue, green
Embroidery stitch: atma stitch
NOTES
Pattern drawn in ink on front
face of fabric; embroidered after
assembly

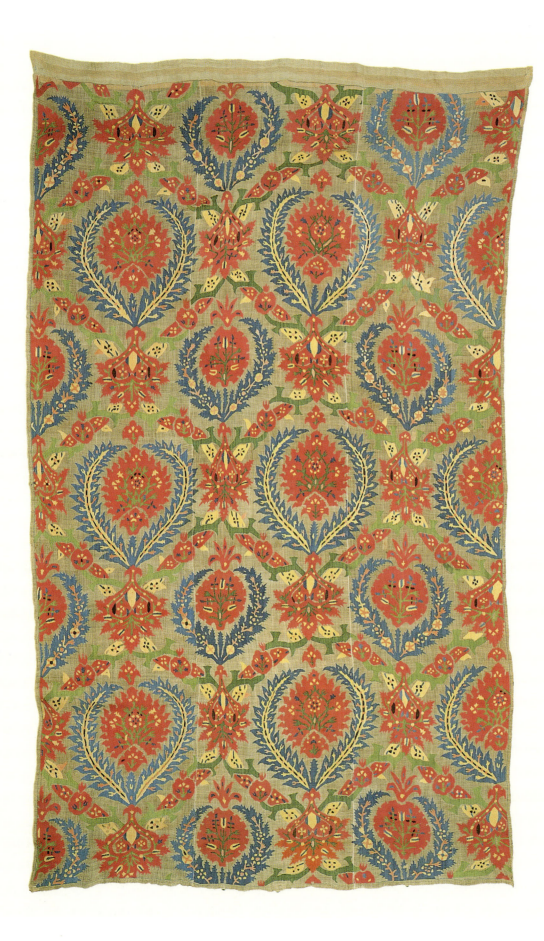

3

Cover
17th century
The Textile Museum 1.42
Acquired by George Hewitt
Myers in 1927
FOUNDATION
Warp: linen, Z-spun, 17/cm,
undyed
Weft: linen, Z-spun, 13/cm,
undyed
Structure: balanced plain weave
Dimensions: overall length 256
cm, overall width 160 cm
Construction: three loom-width
panels sewn together, narrow
panel sewn on across top part of
cover
Edge finish: two selvedges, two
sides rolled and hemmed
EMBROIDERY
Embroidery thread: silk, z2s,
seven colors: dark red, red,
green, blue, yellow, light orange,
black
Embroidery stitch: 3/1 running
stitch in diagonal alignment
(warp direction)
NOTES
Pattern drawn in ink on back
face of fabric; embroidered
before assembly

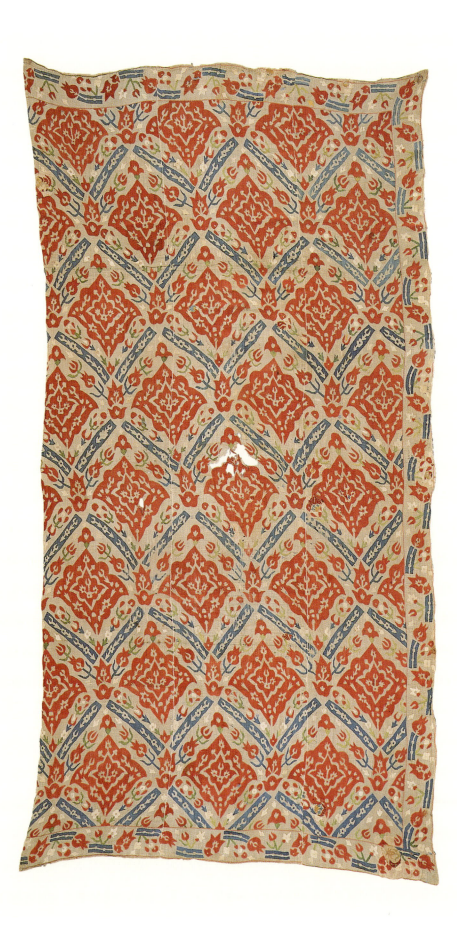

4

Cover
17th century
The Textile Museum 1982.40.3
Gift of Mrs. Charles Putnam

FOUNDATION

Warp: linen, Z-spun, 16/cm, undyed

Weft: linen, Z-spun, 13/cm, undyed

Structure: balanced plain weave

Dimensions: overall length 317 cm, overall width 163 cm

Construction: three loom-width panels sewn together

Edge finish: two selvedges, two sides rolled and hemmed

EMBROIDERY

Embroidery thread: silk, s2z, four colors: red, blue, green, white

Embroidery stitch: 3/1 running stitch in diagonal alignment (warp and weft directions)

NOTES

Stamp (seven-sided) with Arabic inscription at upper right corner on front face of cover; embroidered before assembly

5
Cover fragment
17th century
The Textile Museum 1.41
Acquired by George Hewitt
Myers in 1932
FOUNDATION
Warp: linen, Z-spun, 17/cm,
undyed
Weft: linen, Z-spun, 16/cm,
undyed
Structure: balanced plain weave
Dimensions: overall length
131 cm, overall width 54.5 cm
Edge finish: one selvedge, two
sides rolled and hemmed, one
side cut
EMBROIDERY
Embroidery thread: silk, z2s,
seven colors: red, blue, green,
dark brown, light yellow, white,
dark blue
Embroidery stitches: 5/1 running
stitch in diagonal alignment (weft
direction), chain stitch
NOTES
Pattern drawn in ink on back
face of fabric

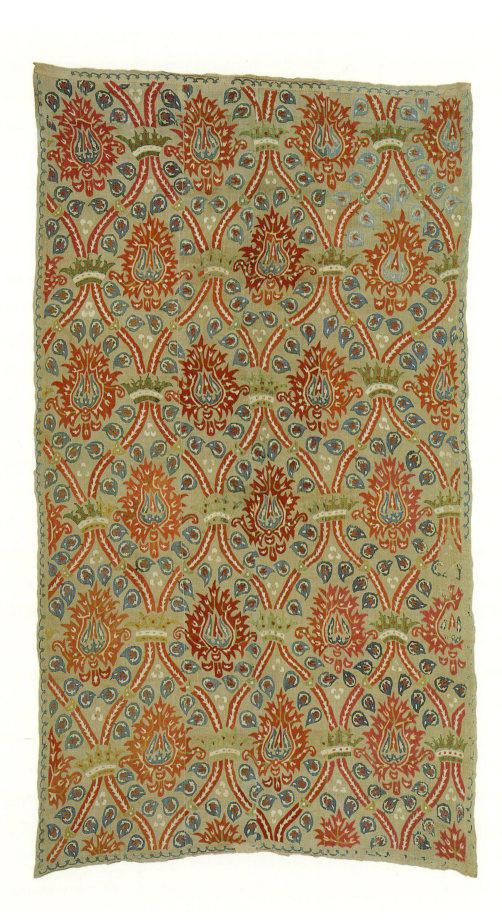

6

Cover
17th century
The Textile Museum 1.8
Acquired by George Hewitt
Myers before 1940
FOUNDATION
Warp: linen, Z-spun, 17/cm,
undyed
Weft: linen, Z-spun, 21/cm,
undyed
Structure: balanced plain weave
Dimensions: overall length
275 cm, overall width 164 cm
Construction: four panels (two
loom-width) sewn together
Edge finish: two selvedges, two
sides rolled and hemmed
EMBROIDERY
Embroidery thread: silk, z2s, six
colors: red, dark red, blue, green,
white, pink
Embroidery stitch: 3/1 running
stitch in diagonal alignment
(warp and weft directions)
NOTES
Pattern drawn in ink on back
face of fabric; embroidered
before assembly

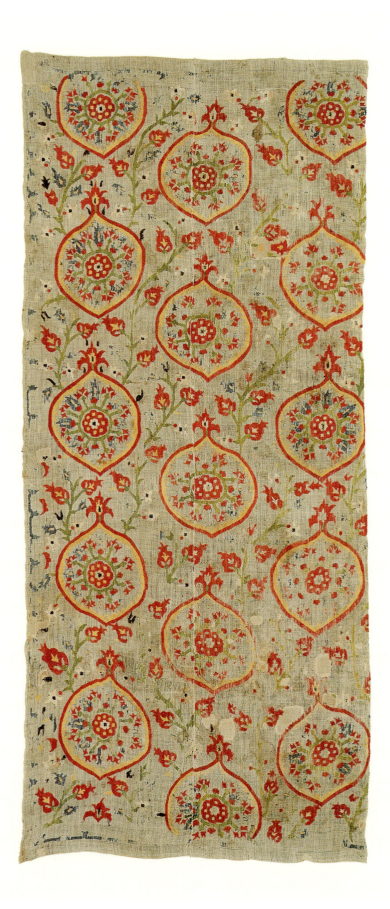

7

Cover fragment (far left)
17th century
The Textile Museum 1.20
Acquired by George Hewitt
Myers before 1940
FOUNDATION
Warp: linen, Z-spun, 14/cm,
undyed
Weft: linen, Z-spun, 10/cm,
undyed
Structure: balanced plain weave
Dimensions: overall length
200 cm, overall width 92 cm
Construction: two loom-width
panels sewn together
Edge finish: one selvedge, three
sides rolled and hemmed
EMBROIDERY
Embroidery thread: silk, z2s,
seven colors: green, blue, red,
yellow, black (dark brown?),
white, light orange
Embroidery stitch: 3/1 running
stitch in diagonal alignment
(warp direction)
NOTES
Pattern drawn in ink on back
face of fabric; embroidered
before assembly; possibly part of
The Textile Museum 1.9

8

Cover fragment (left)
17th century
The Textile Museum 1.9
Acquired by George Hewitt
Myers before 1956
FOUNDATION
Warp: linen, Z-spun, 14/cm,
undyed
Weft: linen, Z-spun, 9/cm,
undyed
Structure: balanced plain weave
Dimensions: overall length
185.5 cm, overall width 44.5 cm
Edge finish: two selvedges, two
sides rolled and hemmed
EMBROIDERY
Embroidery thread: silk, z2s,
seven colors: dark brown, green,
blue, red, yellow, white,
dark yellow
Embroidery stitch: 3/1 running
stitch in diagonal alignment
(warp direction)
NOTES
Pattern drawn in ink on back
face of fabric; possibly part of
The Textile Museum 1.20

9

Cover fragment (right)
17th century or early 18th century
The Textile Museum 1.22
Acquired by George Hewitt
Myers before 1940
FOUNDATION
Warp: linen, Z-spun, 32/cm,
undyed
Weft: linen, Z-spun, 29/cm,
undyed
Structure: balanced plain weave
Dimensions: overall length
231 cm, overall width 78.7 cm
Edge finish: narrow tape sewn
around edge on back face of fabric
EMBROIDERY
Embroidery thread: silk, z2s, thir-
teen colors: black, red, white, off-
white (ivory), yellow, blue, green,
light green, three shades of light
brown, dark brown, pink
Embroidery stitch: double running
stitch
NOTES
Pattern drawn in ink on back
face of fabric

10

Cover fragment
17th century
The Textile Museum 1994.27.4
Gift of Neutrogena Corporation

FOUNDATION
Warp: linen, Z-spun, 18/cm,
undyed
Weft: linen, Z-spun, 16/cm,
undyed
Structure: balanced plain weave
Dimensions: overall length 56 cm,
overall width 52 cm
Edge finish: two selvedges, one
side rolled and hemmed, one
side cut

EMBROIDERY
Embroidery thread: silk, s2z, five
colors: light blue, dark blue,
green, red, yellow
Embroidery stitch: 3/1 running
stitch in diagonal alignment
(warp and weft directions)

NOTES
Pattern drawn in ink on back
face of fabric

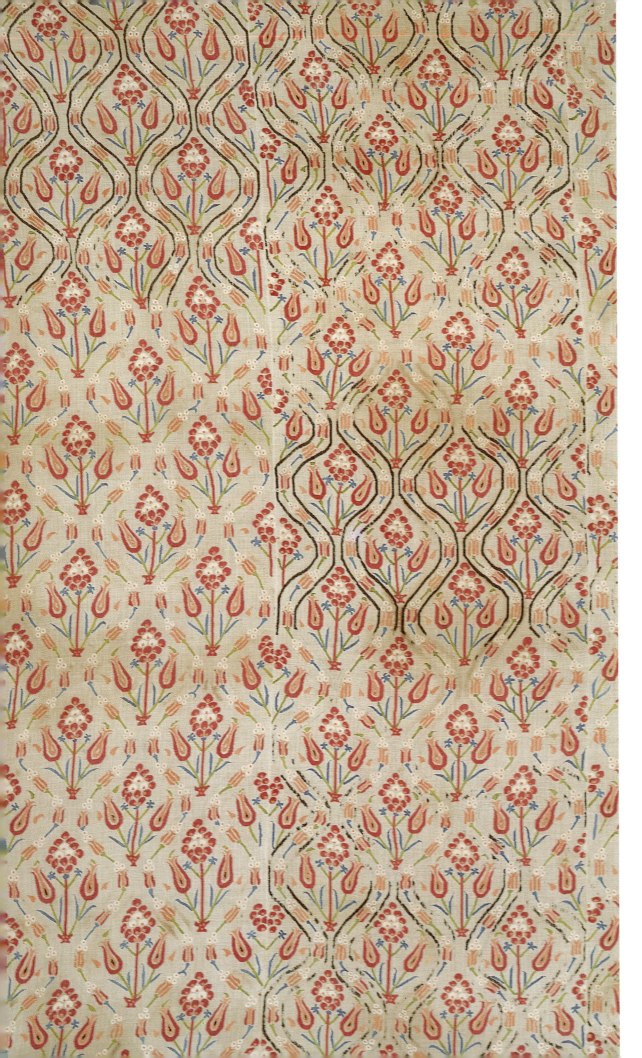

11

Cover
18th century
The Textile Museum 1.37
Acquired by George Hewitt
Myers in 1930

FOUNDATION
Warp: linen, Z-spun, 17/cm,
undyed
Weft: linen, Z-spun, 15/cm,
undyed
Structure: balanced plain weave
Dimensions: overall length
244 cm, overall width 195 cm
Construction: three panels (two
loom-width) sewn together
Edge finish: one selvedge, three
sides rolled and hemmed

EMBROIDERY
Embroidery thread: silk, s2z, six
colors: red, light orange, white,
black, light blue, green
Embroidery stitches: 3/1 running
stitch in diagonal alignment
(warp direction), double running
stitch

NOTES
Pattern drawn in ink on back
face of fabric; embroidered
before assembly

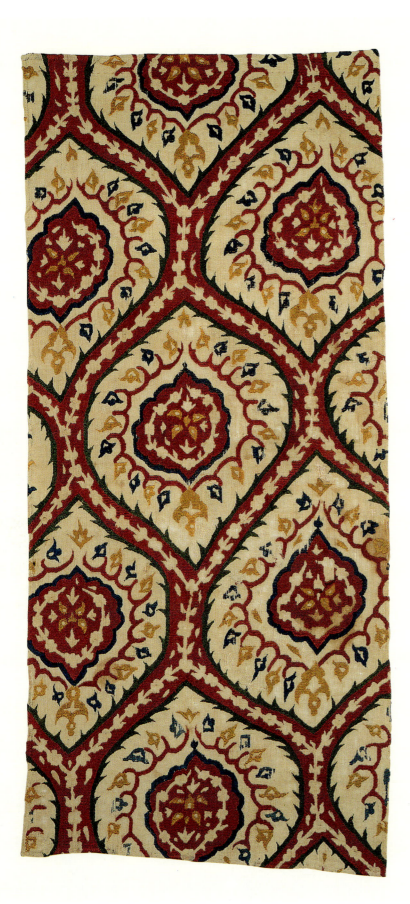

12

Cover fragment
18th century
The Textile Museum 1.14
Acquired by George Hewitt
Myers before 1956

FOUNDATION

Warp: linen, Z-spun, 18/cm,
undyed
Weft: linen, Z-spun, 16/cm,
undyed
Structure: balanced plain weave
Dimensions: overall length
92.5 cm, overall width 44 cm
Edge finish: one selvedge, three
sides rolled and hemmed

EMBROIDERY

Embroidery thread: silk, z2s, four
colors: dark red, green, dark
blue, yellow
Embroidery stitch: 5/1 running
stitch in diagonal alignment
(warp direction)

13

Cover fragment (left)
18th century
The Textile Museum 1.40
Acquired by George Hewitt
Myers in 1934
FOUNDATION
Warp: linen, Z-spun, 20/cm,
undyed
Weft: linen, Z-spun, 17/cm,
undyed
Structure: balanced plain weave
Dimensions: overall length 111 cm,
overall width 42.5 cm
Edge finish: one side rolled and
hemmed, three sides cut
EMBROIDERY
Embroidery thread: silk, s2z, two
colors: red, blue
Embroidery stitches: 5/1 running
stitch in diagonal alignment (weft
direction), chain stitch
NOTES
Pattern drawn in ink on back
face of fabric

14

Cover (right)
18th century
The Textile Museum 1.5
Acquired by George Hewitt
Myers in 1926
FOUNDATION
Warp: linen, Z-spun, 15/cm,
undyed
Weft: linen, Z-spun, 16/cm,
undyed
Structure: balanced plain weave
Dimensions: overall length
245 cm, overall width 126 cm
Construction: three panels sewn
together
Edge finish: two selvedges, two
sides rolled and hemmed
EMBROIDERY
Embroidery thread: silk, z2s, five
colors: red, blue, yellow, black
(dark brown?), green
Embroidery stitches: 4/1 running
stitch in diagonal alignment
(warp and weft directions), chain
stitch
NOTES
Stamp with Arabic script at corner
of back face of cover; pattern
drawn in ink on back face of
fabric; embroidered before
assembly

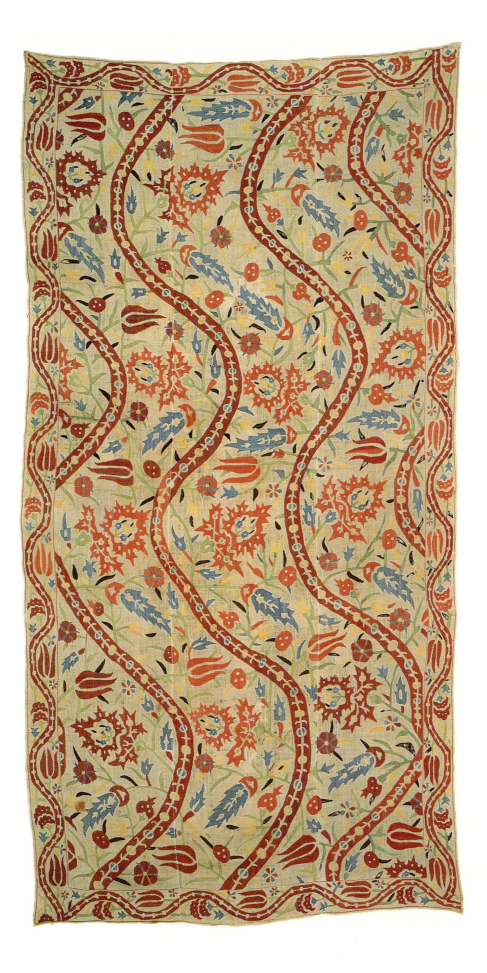

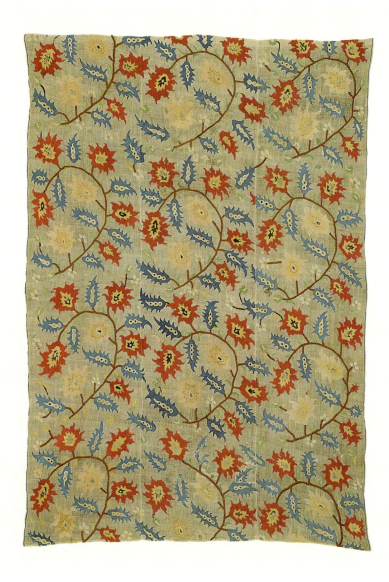

15

Cover fragment
18th century
The Textile Museum 1.13
Acquired by George Hewitt
Myers before 1956

FOUNDATION

Warp: linen, Z-spun, 15/cm,
undyed
Weft: linen, Z-spun, 14/cm,
undyed
Structure: balanced plain weave
Dimensions: overall length 196
cm, overall width 136 cm
Construction: three loom-width
panels sewn together
Edge finish: two selvedges, two
sides rolled and hemmed

EMBROIDERY

Embroidery thread: silk, z2s and
3z2s, six colors: red, light blue,
light green, white, yellow, dark
brown (later addition to replace
disintegrating dark brown
thread)
Embroidery stitches: triangular
Turkish stitch, double running
stitch, herringbone stitch, fishbone stitch

NOTES

Embroidered before assembly

16
Cover (left)
18th century
The Textile Museum 1982.40.2
Gift of Mrs. Charles Putnam
FOUNDATION
Warp: linen, Z-spun, 16/cm, undyed
Weft: linen, Z-spun, 15/cm, undyed
Structure: balanced plain weave
Dimensions: overall length 226 cm,
overall width 127 cm
Construction: three panels sewn
together
Edge finish: two selvedges, two sides
rolled and hemmed
EMBROIDERY
Embroidery threads:
Silk, unspun, six colors: red, dark red,
pink, orange, light blue, dark green
Silk, z2s eight colors: red, dark red,
pink, orange, light blue, dark blue,
dark green, brown (generally for
outlines)
Embroidery stitches: atma stitch,
double running stitch, herringbone
stitch
NOTES
Pattern drawn in ink on front face of
fabric; embroidered after assembly

17
Turban cover (right)
18th century
The Textile Museum 1.36
Acquired by George Hewitt Myers
before 1956
FOUNDATION
Warp: linen, Z-spun, 15/cm, undyed
Selvedge warp: linen, z2s, undyed
Weft: linen, Z-spun, 16/cm, undyed
Structure: balanced plain weave
Dimensions: overall length 104 cm,
overall width 96 cm
Construction: two panels sewn
together
Edge finish: two selvedges, two sides
rolled and hemmed
EMBROIDERY
Embroidery thread: silk, z2s, nine
colors: red, light blue, blue, green,
light green, light brown, white, off-
white (ivory), black
Embroidery stitch: triangular Turkish
stitch
NOTES
Pattern drawn in ink on front face of
fabric; embroidered after assembly

18

Turban cover
Late 18th century
The Textile Museum 1.17
Acquired by George Hewitt
Myers before 1940
FOUNDATION
Warp: linen, Z-spun, 17/cm,
undyed
Weft: linen, Z-spun, 15/cm,
undyed
Structure: balanced plain weave
Dimensions: overall length
105 cm, overall width 119 cm
Construction: two panels sewn
together
Edge finish: one selvedge, three
sides rolled and hemmed
EMBROIDERY
Embroidery threads:
Metallic-wrapped thread: gold-
colored metal strips S-twisted
around yellow silk thread
Silk, z2s, blue
Embroidery stitch: 6/2 running
stitch in diagonal alignment
(warp direction)
NOTES
Embroidered after assembly

19

Turban cover
Second half 18th century
The Textile Museum 1.21
Acquired by George Hewitt
Myers before 1940
FOUNDATION
Warp: linen, Z-spun, 16/cm,
undyed
Weft: linen, Z-spun, 16/cm,
undyed
Structure: balanced plain weave
Dimensions: overall length 92 cm,
overall width 102 cm
Construction: two panels sewn
together
Edge finish: one selvedge, three
sides rolled and hemmed
EMBROIDERY
Embroidery threads:
Silk, z2s, five colors: pink, blue,
green, light brown, dark yellow
Metallic-wrapped thread: gold-
colored metal strips Z-twisted
around light-yellow silk thread
Embroidery stitches: double run-
ning stitch, satin stitch, woven
hem stitch
NOTES
Pattern drawn in ink on front
face of fabric; embroidered after
assembly

20

Bohça (wrapping cloth)
18th century
The Textile Museum 1.7
Acquired by George Hewitt
Myers in 1922
FOUNDATION
Warp: linen, Z-spun, 16/cm, red
Weft: linen, Z-spun, 16/cm, red
Structure: balanced plain weave
Dimensions: overall length 107
cm, overall width 111.5 cm
Construction: one loom-width
panel and one half loom-width
panel sewn together
Edge finish: one selvedge, three
sides rolled and hemmed
EMBROIDERY
Embroidery threads:
Silk, unspun, three colors: blue,
white, light brown
Silk, s2z, four colors: blue, light
brown, white, green
Embroidery stitches: atma stitch,
double running stitch, herring-
bone stitch
NOTES
Pattern drawn in ink on front
face of fabric; embroidered after
assembly

21

Bohça (wrapping cloth)
18th century
The Textile Museum 1.29
Acquired by George Hewitt
Myers before 1956
FOUNDATION
Warp: linen, Z-spun, 16/cm, red
Weft: linen, Z-spun, 16/cm, red
Structure: balanced plain weave
Dimensions: overall length 117
cm, overall width 117 cm
Construction: two panels sewn
together; fully lined with light
blue cotton fabric
EMBROIDERY
Embroidery threads:
Silk, unspun, eight colors: red,
white, light brown, dark blue, blue,
blue-green, green, light green
Silk, z2s, eight colors: red, white,
light brown, dark blue, blue,
blue-green, green, light green
Embroidery stitches: atma stitch,
chain stitch
NOTES
Pattern drawn in ink on front
face of fabric; embroidered after
assembly

22

Bohça (wrapping cloth)
Late 19th century
The Textile Museum 1962.46.1
Gift of Jamal Muzaffar

FOUNDATION

Warp: cotton, Z-spun, brown
Supplementary warp pile: cotton, dark red
Weft: cotton, Z-spun, brown
Structure: velvet
Dimensions: overall length 91 cm, overall width 86.5 cm
Construction: three panels sewn together; fully lined with light-red cotton fabric

EMBROIDERY

Embroidery materials: metallic-wrapped thread, cotton, *tırtıl*, sequins, paper
Embroidery threads:
Metallic-wrapped thread: gold-colored metal strips S-twisted around yellow silk thread
Cotton, z2s, light red
Embroidery: dival embroidery

NOTES

Embroidered after assembly

23
Çevre (headscarf; top left)
Late 18th century
The Textile Museum 1990.4.31
Gift of Leila F. Wilson
FOUNDATION
Warp and weft: linen, Z-spun,
28 × 34/cm, undyed
Structure: balanced plain weave
Dimensions: overall length 86
cm, overall width 86 cm
Edge finish: all four sides rolled
and hemmed
EMBROIDERY
Embroidery threads:
Silk, z2s, eleven colors: orange,
red, pink, purple, dark brown,
light brown, green, two shades
of light green, dark green, blue
Metal strips, gold- and silver-
colored
Embroidery stitches: double run-
ning stitch, satin stitch, *muşabak*
stitch

24
Çevre (headscarf; bottom left)
Late 18th century
The Textile Museum 1986.22.1
Gift of Mr. and Mrs. Anthony
Geber
FOUNDATION
Warp and weft: linen, Z-spun,
23 × 23/cm, undyed
Structure: balanced plain weave
Dimensions: overall length 99
cm, overall width 94 cm
Edge finish: needle lace edging
with metal strips
EMBROIDERY
Embroidery threads:
Silk, z2s, nine colors: three
shades of light green, two shades
of blue, two shades of light blue,
white, light brown
Metal strips, gold-colored
Metallic-wrapped thread: gold-
colored metal strips Z-twisted
around z3s undyed cotton
thread
Embroidery stitches: double running stitch, satin stitch, *muşabak*
stitch

25
Çevre (headscarf; detail, top)
Late 18th or early 19th century
The Textile Museum 1974.11.7
Gift of Walter D. Addison
FOUNDATION
Warp and weft: cotton, Z-spun,
24 × 28/cm, undyed
Structure: balanced plain weave
Dimensions: overall length 87
cm, overall width 82 cm
Edge finish: scalloped and edged
with buttonhole stitch
EMBROIDERY
Embroidery threads:
Silk, z2s, four colors: blue, light
blue, white, dark green
Metallic-wrapped thread: gold-
colored metal strips S-twisted
around yellow and light-yellow
silk thread
Embroidery stitches: satin stitch,
buttonhole stitch, eyelet stitch

26
Çevre (headscarf; detail, bottom)
Late 19th century
The Textile Museum 1999.18.6
Gift of David Dew Bruner
FOUNDATION
Warp and weft: linen, Z-spun,
24 × 18/cm, undyed
Structure: balanced plain weave
Dimensions: overall length
78 cm, overall width 76 cm
Edge finish: crochet around all
edges
EMBROIDERY
Embroidery threads:
Silk, z2s, five colors: red, pink,
brown, off-white (ivory), light
orange
Metallic-wrapped thread: gold-
colored metal strips Z-twisted
around light-yellow silk thread
Embroidery stitches: double run-
ning stitch, satin stitch, eyelet
stitch

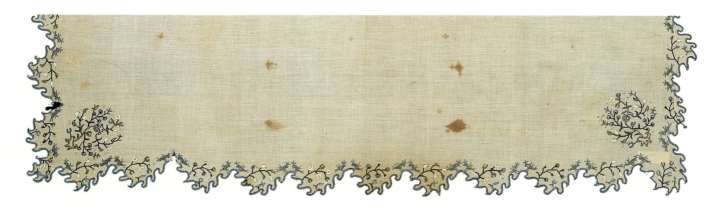

27

Mirror cover
Early 18th century
The Textile Museum 1.31
Acquired by George Hewitt
Myers before 1956
FOUNDATION
Warp: linen, Z-spun, 15/cm,
undyed
Weft: linen, Z-spun, 16/cm,
undyed
Structure: balanced plain weave
Dimensions: overall length 137
cm, overall width 51 cm
Construction: a portion of narrow
end shortened
Edge finish: two selvedges, two
sides rolled and hemmed
EMBROIDERY
Embroidery thread: silk, z2s, six
colors: blue, white, light brown,
light green, dark pink (faded),
dark yellow
Embroidery stitches: double run-
ning stitch, Romanian self-
couching stitch, satin stitch

28

Mirror cover (detail)
Early 18th century
The Textile Museum 1.32
Acquired by George Hewitt
Myers before 1940

FOUNDATION

Warp: linen, Z-spun, 19/cm,
undyed
Weft: linen, Z-spun, 15/cm,
undyed
Structure: balanced plain weave
Dimensions: overall length
137 cm, overall width 51 cm
Edge finish: two selvedges, two
warp fringes

EMBROIDERY

Embroidery thread: silk, z2s, nine
colors: red, light blue, white, light
brown, green, light green, dark
brown, pink (faded), off-white
(ivory)
Embroidery stitches: double running stitch, satin stitch

29

Mirror cover
Early 18th century
The Textile Museum 1.10
Acquired by George Hewitt
Myers in 1916

FOUNDATION
Warp: linen, Z-spun, 18/cm,
undyed
Weft: linen, Z-spun, 16/cm,
undyed
Structure: balanced plain weave
Dimensions: overall length 130
cm, overall width 52 cm
Edge finish: two selvedges, two
sides rolled and hemmed

EMBROIDERY
Embroidery thread: silk, z2s, five
colors: red, light blue, light green,
light brown, off-white (ivory)
Embroidery stitches: double running stitch worked with alternating straight and stepped versions
of the stitch, satin stitch

NOTES
Pattern drawn in ink on front
face of fabric

30

Yağlık (napkin)
19th century
The Textile Museum 1975.14.2
Gift of Leila F. Wilson
FOUNDATION
Warp: linen, Z-spun, 27/cm,
undyed
Weft: linen, Z-spun, 27/cm,
undyed
Structure: balanced plain weave
Dimensions: overall length
146.5 cm, overall width 50 cm
Edge finish: one selvedge, three
sides rolled and hemmed; cro-
chet edging around the embroi-
dered end panels
EMBROIDERY
Embroidery threads:
Silk, z2s, nine colors: red, pink,
two shades of light brown, light
blue, purple, two shades of light
green, dark green
Metallic-wrapped thread: gold-
colored metal strips Z-twisted
around light-yellow silk thread
Metal strips, gold-colored
Embroidery stitches: double running stitch, satin stitch
NOTES
Pattern drawn in ink on back
face of fabric

31

Yağlık (napkin)
19th century
The Textile Museum 1979.22.2
Gift of Mrs. Harold B. Hoskins

FOUNDATION

Warp: linen, Z-spun, 20/cm,
undyed
Weft: linen, Z-spun, 23/cm,
undyed
Structure: balanced plain weave
Dimensions: overall length
71.5 cm, overall width 55 cm
Edge finish: two selvedges, two
sides rolled and hemmed; crochet
edging around the embroidered
end panels

EMBROIDERY

Embroidery threads:
Silk, z2s, sixteen colors: light
blue, blue, green, light green,
dark green, two shades of brown,
two shades of light brown, dark
brown, yellow, orange, red, pink,
white, gray
Metallic-wrapped thread:
gold-colored metal strips Z-
twisted around light-yellow silk
thread
Metallic-wrapped thread: silver-
colored metal strips Z-twisted
around white silk thread
Metal strips, gold-colored
Embroidery stitches: double
running stitch, satin stitch,
muşabak stitch

NOTES

Pattern drawn in ink on front
face of fabric

32

Yağlık (napkin)
19th century
The Textile Museum 1990.4.30
Gift of Leila F. Wilson
FOUNDATION
Warp: cotton, Z-spun, 23/cm,
undyed
Weft: cotton, Z-spun, 22/cm,
undyed
Structure: balanced plain weave
Dimensions: overall length
127 cm, overall width 50 cm
Edge finish: one selvedge, three
sides rolled and hemmed
EMBROIDERY
Embroidery threads:
Silk, z2s, eleven colors: three
shades of light green, three
shades of light brown, light blue,
blue, white, pink, red
Metallic-wrapped thread: gold-
colored metal strips Z-twisted
around light-yellow silk thread
Silk, 2s, light yellow (used only
on sections where metal strips
applied)
Metal strips, gold colored
Embroidery stitches: double running stitch, satin stitch
NOTES
Pattern drawn in ink on front
face of fabric

33

Yağlık (napkin)
19th century
The Textile Museum 1990.4.33
Gift of Leila F. Wilson
FOUNDATION
Warp: cotton, Z-spun, 18/cm,
undyed
Weft: cotton, Z-spun, 19/cm,
undyed
Structure: balanced plain weave
Dimensions: overall length
129 cm, overall width 51 cm
Edge finish: one selvedge, three
sides rolled and hemmed; cro-
chet edging around the embroi-
dered end panels
EMBROIDERY
Embroidery threads:
Silk, z2s, nine colors: red, pink,
light blue, blue, off-white (ivory),
two shades of light green, green,
light brown
Metallic-wrapped thread: gold-
colored metal strips Z-twisted
around light-yellow silk thread
Metal strips, gold-colored
Embroidery stitches: double running stitch, satin stitch, *muşabak*
stitch
NOTES
Two types of metallic-wrapped
threads were used in this piece.
In one type, used for the crochet
edging, metal strips were tightly
twisted around the silk thread.
The other thread was made out
of metal strips loosely twisted
around silk thread, exposing
some of the silk; this was used
for the embroidery.

34

Yağlık (napkin)
19th century
The Textile Museum 1983.59.9
Gift of John Davis Hatch in
memory of Anna Van Scheick
Mitchell

FOUNDATION

Warp: linen, Z-spun, 34/cm,
undyed
Weft: linen, Z-spun, 34/cm,
undyed
Structure: balanced plain weave
Dimensions: overall length
157 cm, overall width 51 cm
Edge finish: one selvedge, three
sides rolled and hemmed; crochet edging around the embroidered end panels

EMBROIDERY

Embroidery threads:
Silk, s2z, eight colors: red, pink,
two shades of light blue, green,
two shades of light green, light
brown
Metallic-wrapped thread: gold-
colored metal strips Z-twisted
around light-yellow silk thread
Metal strips, gold-colored
Embroidery stitches: double
running stitch, satin stitch

NOTES

Pattern drawn in ink on front
face of fabric. Two types of
metallic-wrapped threads were
used for this embroidery: in one,
gold-colored metal strips were
tightly twisted around silk
thread; the other thread was
made out of metal strips loosely
twisted around the silk thread,
exposing some of the silk.

35

Yağlık (napkin; detail)
19th century
The Textile Museum 1985.33.166
Gift of The Florence Eddowes
Morris Collection, Goucher
College

FOUNDATION

Warp: linen, Z-spun, 23/cm,
undyed
Weft: linen, Z-spun, 23/cm,
undyed
Structure: balanced plain weave
Dimensions: overall length
144 cm, overall width 52.5 cm
Edge finish: two selvedges, two
sides rolled and hemmed; crochet edging around the embroidered end panels

EMBROIDERY

Embroidery threads:
Silk, z2s and s2z, sixteen colors:
four shades of green, red, two
shades of pink, light orange, yellow, light yellow, off-white
(white), blue, two shades of light
brown, dark brown, purple
Metallic-wrapped thread: gold-
colored metal strips Z-twisted
around light-yellow silk thread
Metallic-wrapped thread: silver-
colored metal strips Z-twisted
around white silk thread
Metal strips, gold-colored
Embroidery stitches: double running stitch, satin stitch, *muşabak*
stitch

36

Yağlık (napkin)
19th century
The Textile Museum 1999.18.5
Gift of David Dew Bruner

FOUNDATION

Warp: cotton, Z-spun, 20/cm, undyed
Weft: cotton, Z-spun, 26/cm, undyed
Structure: balanced plain weave
Dimensions: overall length 163.5 cm, overall width 82 cm
Edge finish: two selvedges, two sides rolled and hemmed; crochet edging around the embroidered end panels

EMBROIDERY

Embroidery threads:
Silk, z2s, thirteen colors: blue, light blue, red, two shades of green, three shades of light green, gray, pink, two shades of light brown, brown
Metallic-wrapped thread: gold-colored metal strips Z-twisted around light yellow silk thread
Metallic-wrapped thread: gold-colored metal strips S-twisted around light-yellow silk thread (used in crochet edging)
Embroidery stitches: double running stitch, satin stitch, *muşabak* stitch

37
Yağlık (napkin; top)
19th century
The Textile Museum 1983.59.8
Gift of John Davis Hatch in
memory of Anna Van Scheick
Mitchell
FOUNDATION
Warp: linen, Z-spun, 18/cm,
undyed
Weft: linen, Z-spun, 26/cm,
undyed
Structure: balanced plain weave
Dimensions: overall length
136 cm, overall width 47 cm
Edge finish: one selvedge, three
sides rolled and hemmed; crochet edging around the embroidered end panels
EMBROIDERY
Embroidery threads:
Silk, z2s, thirteen colors: red,
pink, two shades of dark brown,
light brown, red-brown, green,
two shades of light green, light
orange, off-white (ivory), light
blue, dark blue
Metallic-wrapped thread: gold-
colored metal strips Z-twisted
around light-yellow silk thread
Metallic-wrapped thread: silver-
colored metal strips Z-twisted
around white silk thread
Embroidery stitches: double running stitch, satin stitch, fishbone
stitch

38
Yağlık (napkin; bottom)
Late 19th or early 20th century
The Textile Museum 1985.33.165
Gift of The Florence Eddowes
Morris Collection, Goucher
College
FOUNDATION
Warp: cotton, Z-spun, 18/cm,
undyed
Weft: cotton, Z-spun, 18/cm,
undyed
Structure: balanced plain weave
Dimensions: overall length
148 cm, overall width 52 cm
Edge finish: one selvedge, three
sides rolled and hemmed; cro-
chet edging around the embroi-
dered end panels
EMBROIDERY
Embroidery threads:
Silk, z2s, seventeen colors: dark
red, red, pink, light pink, orange,
light orange, two shades of light
purple, blue-green, blue, two
shades of dark blue, dark green,
green, light green, light yellow,
brown
Metallic-wrapped thread: gold-
colored metal strips Z-twisted
around light-yellow silk thread
Embroidery stitches: double running stitch, satin stitch, stem
stitch

39

Yağlık (napkin)
19th century
The Textile Museum 1979.22.1
Gift of Mrs. Harold B. Hoskins

FOUNDATION
Warp: cotton, Z-spun, 24/cm, undyed
Weft: cotton, Z-spun, 30/cm, undyed
Structure: balanced plain weave
Dimensions: overall length 102.5 cm, overall width 51.5 cm
Edge finish: one selvedge, three sides rolled and hemmed; crochet edging around the embroidered end panels

EMBROIDERY
Embroidery threads:
Silk, z2s, six colors: red, pink, light green, green, blue, off-white (ivory)
Metallic-wrapped thread: gold-colored metal strips Z-twisted around light-yellow silk thread
Metallic-wrapped thread: silver-colored metal strips Z-twisted around white silk thread
Embroidery stitch: double running stitch

40

Hearth cover
Early 19th century
The Textile Museum 1999.18.1
Gift of David Dew Bruner
FOUNDATION
Warp: silk, unspun, light brown
Weft: silk, unspun, pink (faded
from dark pink)
Structure: satin weave
Dimensions: overall length 73 cm,
overall width 120 cm
Construction: fully lined with
yellow silk fabric
EMBROIDERY
Embroidery threads:
Silk, s2z, yellow
Metallic-wrapped thread: gold-
colored metal strips Z-twisted
around light-yellow silk thread
Embroidery technique: couching

41

Tray cover
19th century
The Textile Museum 1965.14.1
Gift of Mrs. Fred S. Gichner
FOUNDATION
Warp: silk, black
Weft: silk, dark brown
Structure: satin weave
Dimensions: overall diameter
140 cm
EMBROIDERY
Embroidery materials: sequins,
silk, metal wire
Embroidery threads:
Silk, s2z, dark yellow
Metal wire: two groups of three
wires Z-plied, gold
Embroidery technique: couching

42

Namazlık (prayer cloth)
1910–1925
The Textile Museum 1999.4.1
Gift of Mrs. Jale Çolakoğlu
FOUNDATION
Supplementary warp pile: cotton,
dark red
Structure: velvet
Dimensions: overall length
132 cm, overall width 86 cm
Construction: two panels sewn
together; fully lined with blue
cotton fabric
Edge finish: applied trim band
EMBROIDERY
Embroidery materials: metallic-
wrapped thread, cotton, sequins,
tırtıl
Embroidery threads:
Metallic-wrapped thread: gold-
colored metal strips S-twisted
around light-yellow silk thread
Cotton, z2s, white
Embroidery style: dival
NOTES
Embroidered after assembly

43

Apron from a barber's set
19th century
The Textile Museum 1985.48.1a
Gift of Mr. and Mrs. William O.
Baxter

FOUNDATION

Warp: cotton, Z-spun, white
Weft: cotton, Z-spun, white
Structure: balanced plain weave
Dimensions: overall length
165 cm, overall width 111 cm
Edge finish: applied band crocheted with metallic-wrapped
thread

EMBROIDERY

Embroidery threads:
Silk, unspun, six colors: red,
pink, light green, green, blue,
off-white (ivory)
Metallic-wrapped thread: gold-colored metal strips Z-twisted
around light-yellow silk thread
(used in crochet edging)
Embroidery stitch: chain stitch

44

Towel from a barber's set
19th century
The Textile Museum 1985.48.1b
Gift of Mr. and Mrs. William O.
Baxter

FOUNDATION

Warp: cotton, Z-spun, white
Weft: cotton, Z-spun, white
Structure: balanced plain weave
Dimensions: overall length
102.5 cm, overall width 54 cm
Edge finish: applied band
crocheted with metallic-wrapped
thread

EMBROIDERY

Embroidery threads:
Silk, unspun, six colors: red,
pink, light green, green, blue, off-white (ivory)
Metallic-wrapped thread: gold-colored metal strips Z-twisted
around light-yellow silk thread
(used in crochet edging)
Embroidery stitch: chain stitch

45

Towel fragment
Late 18th or early 19th century
The Textile Museum 1999.18.4
Gift of David Dew Bruner
FOUNDATION
Warp: linen, Z-spun, undyed
Weft: linen, Z-spun, undyed
Structure: 2/2 twill weave with
supplementary warp loops
Dimensions: overall length 96 cm,
overall width 90 cm
Edge finish: two selvedges, one
warp fringe, one edge rolled and
hemmed
EMBROIDERY
Embroidery threads:
Silk, z2s, twelve colors: red, pink,
light pink, light green, green,
light brown, blue, light blue,
blue-green, dark yellow, off-
white (ivory), light orange
Metallic-wrapped thread: gold-
colored metal strips Z-twisted
around yellow silk thread
Metal strips, gold-colored
Embroidery stitches: double running stitch, satin stitch

46

Towel (detail)
19th century
The Textile Museum 1999.18.11
Gift of David Dew Bruner
FOUNDATION
Warp: linen, Z-spun, undyed
Weft: linen, Z-spun, undyed
Structure: 2/2 twill weave with
supplementary warp loops
Dimensions: overall length
168 cm, overall width 86 cm
Edge finish: two selvedges, two
warp fringes
EMBROIDERY
Embroidery threads:
Silk, z2s, z5s and z3s, nine colors:
two shades of light pink, green,
light green, blue, light blue,
brown, two shades of light brown
Metallic-wrapped thread: gold-
colored metal strips Z-twisted
around yellow silk thread
Embroidery stitches: double run-
ning stitch, satin stitch
NOTES
Manufacturer's mark woven into
one of the ends

47
Uçkur (sash; detail)
Early 18th century
The Textile Museum 1.2
Acquired by George Hewitt
Myers in 1925
FOUNDATION
Warp: linen, Z-spun, 19/cm,
undyed
Weft: linen, Z-spun, 15/cm,
undyed
Structure: balanced plain weave
Dimensions: overall length
193 cm, overall width 45.5 cm
Edge finish: two selvedges, two
warp fringes
EMBROIDERY
Embroidery thread: silk, z2s, eight
colors: blue, red, light red, green,
light yellow, black, light brown,
white
Embroidery stitches: double run-
ning stitch, satin stitch

48

Uçkur (sash; detail)
18th century
The Textile Museum 1996.27.1
Gift of David Dew Bruner
FOUNDATION
Warp: linen, Z-spun, 19/cm,
undyed
Weft: linen, Z-spun, 22/cm,
undyed
Structure: balanced plain weave
Dimensions: overall length
199.5 cm, overall width 24 cm
Edge finish: one selvedge, three
sides rolled and hemmed
EMBROIDERY
Embroidery threads:
Silk, z2s, five colors: pink, light
blue, light green, dark reddish
purple, brown
Metallic-wrapped thread: gold-
colored metal strips S-twisted
around light green and dark-yellow silk threads
Metallic-wrapped thread: silver-
colored metal strips S-twisted
around white silk thread
Embroidery stitches: double running stitch, satin stitch, fishbone
stitch

49

Uçkur (sash; detail)
19th century
The Textile Museum 1999.18.2
Gift of David Dew Bruner
FOUNDATION
Warp: linen, Z-spun, 26/cm,
undyed
Weft: linen, Z-spun, 20/cm,
undyed
Structure: balanced plain weave
Dimensions: overall length
210 cm, overall width 35.5 cm
Edge finish: one selvedge, three
sides rolled and hemmed
EMBROIDERY
Embroidery threads:
Silk, unspun, nine colors: pink,
light yellow, two shades of green,
light green, blue, white, off-white,
light brown
Metallic-wrapped thread: silver-
colored metal strips S-twisted
around off-white silk thread
Embroidery stitches: double running stitch, satin stitch, eyelet
stitch

50

Uçkur (sash; detail)
Late 18th or early 19th century
The Textile Museum 1.88
Gift of Mrs. Hoffman Philip

FOUNDATION

Warp: linen, Z-spun, 42/cm,
undyed
Weft: linen, Z-spun, 36/cm,
undyed
Structure: balanced plain weave
Dimensions: overall length
225 cm, overall width 35 cm
Edge finish: one selvedge, three
sides rolled and hemmed

EMBROIDERY

Embroidery threads:
Silk, z2s, eight colors: red, pink,
yellow, orange, green, purple,
light blue, light green
Metallic-wrapped thread: gold-
colored metal strips Z-twisted
around light-yellow silk thread
Metal strips, gold colored
Embroidery stitches: double running stitch, running stitch, satin
stitch

51

Uçkur (sash; detail, left)
19th century
The Textile Museum 1975.14.3
Gift of Leila F. Wilson
FOUNDATION
Warp: linen, Z-spun, 18/cm, undyed
Weft: linen, Z-spun, 16/cm, undyed
Structure: balanced plain weave
Dimensions: overall length 230 cm, overall width 26 cm
Edge finish: one selvedge, three sides rolled and hemmed
EMBROIDERY
Embroidery threads:
Silk, s2z, eight colors: blue, light blue, light red, pink, light brown, off-white (ivory), green, light green
Metallic-wrapped thread: gold-colored metal strips Z-twisted around light-yellow silk thread
Metal strips, gold colored
Embroidery stitches: double running stitch, satin stitch

52

Uncut *uçkur* (sash; right)
19th century
The Textile Museum 1983.59.6
Gift of John Davis Hatch in memory of Anna Van Scheick Mitchell
FOUNDATION
Warp: linen, Z-spun, 19/cm, undyed
Weft: linen, Z-spun, 22/cm, undyed
Structure: balanced plain weave
Dimensions: overall length 220.5 cm, overall width 42 cm
Edge finish: two selvedges, two sides rolled and hemmed
EMBROIDERY
Embroidery threads:
Silk, z2s, eight colors: blue, light blue, pink, white, green, light brown, off-white, brown
Metallic-wrapped thread: silver-colored metal strips Z-twisted around white silk thread
Embroidery stitches: double running stitch, *muşabak* stitch, crossed stitch

53

Uçkur (sash; detail, far right)
19th century
The Textile Museum 1962.12.2
Gift of Mrs. Gordon W. Phelps
FOUNDATION
Warp: linen, Z-spun, 18/cm, undyed
Selvedge warp: silk, unspun, dark brown
Weft: linen, Z-spun, 18/cm, undyed
Structure: balanced plain weave
Dimensions: overall length 222 cm, overall width 23 cm
Edge finish: two selvedges, two sides rolled and hemmed
EMBROIDERY
Embroidery threads:
Silk, z2s, eleven colors: red, pink, blue, light blue, green, two shades of light green, brown, light brown, gray, off-white (ivory)
Metal strips, silver colored
Embroidery stitches: double running stitch, *muşabak* stitch

54

Uçkur (sash; detail)
19th century
The Textile Museum 1999.18.16
Gift of David Dew Bruner

FOUNDATION

Warp: linen, Z-spun, 19/cm,
undyed
Weft: linen, Z-spun, 15/cm,
undyed
Structure: balanced plain weave
Dimensions: overall length
194 cm, overall width 26 cm
Edge finish: two selvedges, two
sides rolled and hemmed

EMBROIDERY

Embroidery threads:
Silk, z2s, nine colors: green, two
shades of light green, blue, light
blue, red, light brown, pink, reddish purple
Metallic-wrapped thread: gold-
colored metal strips Z-twisted
around light orange silk thread
Embroidery stitches: double running stitch, hem stitch, satin
stitch, *mürver* stitch

NOTES

Pattern drawn in ink on front
face of fabric

55

Uçkur (sash; detail)
19th century
The Textile Museum 1999.18.17
Gift of David Dew Bruner
FOUNDATION
Warp: linen, Z-spun, 17/cm,
undyed
Selvedge warp: silk, unspun,
white
Weft: linen, Z-spun, 15/cm,
undyed
Structure: balanced plain weave
Dimensions: overall length
208 cm, overall width 28 cm
Edge finish: two selvedges, two
sides rolled and hemmed
EMBROIDERY
Embroidery threads:
Silk, z2s, eight colors: green, light
green, pink, two shades of light
brown, off-white (ivory), light
blue, brown
Metallic-wrapped thread: gold-
colored metal strips Z-twisted
around light-yellow silk thread
Embroidery stitches: double running stitch, satin stitch, *mürver*
stitch

56

Bindallı (dress)
Late 19th or early 20th century
The Textile Museum 1978.22
Gift of Mr. Yavuz Sümer
FOUNDATION
Warp: cotton, Z-spun, dark
brown
Supplementary warp pile: silk,
purple
Weft: cotton, Z-spun, dark brown
Structure: velvet
Construction: fully lined with
printed cotton fabric
Dimensions: overall length
139.5 cm, overall width 161 cm
EMBROIDERY
Embroidery materials: metallic-
wrapped thread, cotton, *tırtıl*,
paper
Embroidery threads:
Metallic-wrapped thread: gold-
colored metal strips S-twisted
around dark-yellow silk thread
Cotton, z2s, light red
Embroidery style: dival
NOTES
Applied lace band encircling
neck opening; embroidered after
assembly

57

Slippers
19th century
The Textile Museum 1999.18.10A
and .10B
Gift of David Dew Bruner
FOUNDATION
Structure: velvet
Dimensions: overall length 27 cm
EMBROIDERY
Embroidery materials: metallic-
wrapped thread, *tırtıl*, cotton,
paper
Embroidery threads:
Metallic-wrapped thread: gold-
colored metal strips Z-twisted
around light-yellow silk thread
Cotton, z2s, off-white
Embroidery style: dival

Bibliography

OTTOMAN EMBROIDERY

1998 Embroidery Classification, *Textile Lexicon*. The Lloyd Cotsen Textile Documentation Project. The Textile Museum, Washington.

1978 *İşlemeler: Ottoman Domestic Embroideries*. Exhibition catalog. David Black Oriental Carpets, London.

Baines, Patricia
1989 *Linen: Hand Spinning and Weaving*. B.T. Batsford Ltd., London.

Baker, Patricia L.
1995 *Islamic Textiles*. British Museum Press, London.

Barışta, H. Örçün
1988 *Turkish Handicrafts*, Art Book Series, no. 11. Ministry of Culture and Tourism, Ankara.

1995 *Türk İşleme Sanatı Tarihi*. Second edition. Gazi University Publication, Ankara.

Berker, Nurhayat
1981 *İşlemeler*, Topkapı Sarayı Müzesi, no. 6. Yapı ve Kredi Bankası, İstanbul.

1991? *Türk İşlemeleri* (The Turkish Embroidery). Translated by Virginia Taylor-Saçlıoğlu, photography by Sami Guner. Yapı Kredi Yayınlari Ltd., İstanbul.

Berry, Burton Yost
1932 Old Turkish Towels, *The Art Bulletin*, vol. 14, no. 4, December, pp. 344–58. The College Art Association of America.

1938 Old Turkish Towels II, *The Art Bulletin*, vol. 20, no. 3, September, pp. 251–65. The College Art Association of America.

Celâl, Melek (Lampe)
1939 *Türk İşlemeleri*. Kenan Basıevi ve Klişe Fabrikası, İstanbul.

Delibaş, Selma
1987 Embroidery, *Arts of Weaving, Traditional Turkish Arts*, pp. 47–59. Edited by Dr. Nazan Ölçen. Turkish Republic, Ministry of Culture and Tourism, General Directorate of Fine Arts, Ankara.

Denel, Serim
1992 Statements from the Loom and the Needle: Woven and Embroidered Anatolian Textiles in the Home Environment, *Textiles in Daily Life*. Proceedings of the Third Biennial Symposium of the Textile Society of America, September 24–26, 1992, pp. 249–57.

Denny, Walter
1982 Textiles, *Tulips, Arabesque & Turbans: Decorative Arts from the Ottoman Empire*, pp. 115–59. Edited by Yanni Petsopoulos. Abbeville Press, New York.

Dietrich, Dr. Bernhard
1911 *Kleinasiatische Stickereien*. Dr. Bernhard Dietrich, Plauen.

de Dillmont, Thérèse
1978 *The Complete Encyclopedia of Needlework*. Running Press, Philadelphia.

Ellis, F. Marianne
1989 Turkish Embroidery, *Embroidery*, vol. 40, no. 3, autumn, pp. 138–40.

1992 Metal Thread Embroidery from Ottoman Turkey, *Embroidery*, vol. 43, no. 1, spring, pp. 37–39.

Emery, Irene
1994 *The Primary Structures of Fabrics: An Illustrated Classification*. The Textile Museum, Washington and Watson-Guptill Publications, New York.

Farr, Cheryl Ann
1994 Metallic Yarns: A Technological and Cultural Perspective for the Development of a Morphological Classification System, *Ars Textrina*, vol. 22, December, pp. 65–85. Winnipeg.

Gentles, Margaret
1964 *Turkish and Greek Island Embroideries from the Burton Yost Berry Collection in The Art Institute of Chicago*. The Art Institute of Chicago, Chicago.

Gervers, Veronika
1982 *The Influence of Ottoman Turkish Textiles and Costume in Eastern Europe*. History, Technology, and Art Monograph, no. 4, Royal Ontario Museum, Toronto.

Gönül, Macide
1969 Some Turkish Embroideries in the Collection of the Topkapi Sarayi Museum in Istanbul, *Kunst des Orients*, vol. 6, no. 1, pp. 43–76. Franz Steiner Verlag, Wiesbaden.

1973 *Turkish Embroideries 16th–19th Centuries*. Touring and Automobile Club of Turkey, Ankara.

Helmecke, Gisela
1995 Embroideries, *A Wealth of Silk and Velvet, Ottoman Fabrics and Embroideries*, pp. 25–76. Edited by Christian Erber. Edition Temmen, Bremen.

Johnstone, Pauline
1985 *Turkish Embroidery*. Victoria and Albert Museum, London.

1986 Some Unusual Turkish Embroideries of the Early Eighteenth Century, *The Textile Museum Journal*, vol. 24, 1985, pp. 74–81. Washington.

Lehmberg, Phyllis
1981 Turkish Embroidery, *The Flying Needle*, vol. 10, no. 4, November, pp. 14–16.

Martiniani-Reber, Marielle, Anne Rinuy and Annalisa Galizia
1995 *Çeyiz: Broderies de l'Empire Ottoman*. Musée d'art et d'histoire, Geneva.

Newberry, Essie W.
1936 Turkish Embroidery, *Embroidery, The Journal of the Embroiderers' Guild*, vol. 4, no. 3, June, pp. 48–62.

von Palotay, G.
1954 The Turkish Linen Embroidery, *Ciba Review*, vol. 102, February, pp. 3658–63. Basel.

1954 Motives and Composition, *Ciba Review*, vol. 102, February, pp. 3665–70. Basel.

1954 Embroidery on Velvet, Silk, and Leather, *Ciba Review*, vol. 102, February, pp. 3673–76. Basel.

1954 Turkish Influence in European Embroidery, *Ciba Review*, vol. 102, February, pp. 3678–83. Basel.

Ramazanoğlu, Gülseren
1976 *Turkish Embroidery*. Van Nostrand Reinhold Company, New York, Cincinnati, Toronto, London, Melbourne.

Sürür, Ayten
1976 *Türk İşleme Sanatı*. Ak Yayınları Türk Süsleme Sanatları Serisi, no. 4, İstanbul.

Taylor, Roderick R.
1990 Quilt Facings & Mirror Covers, *Hali*, issue 51, vol. 12, no. 3, June, pp. 118–25. London.

1993 *Ottoman Embroidery*. Marston House, Marston Magna, Yeovil and The Ministry of Culture of the Republic of Turkey, Ankara.

Ther, Ulla
1995 *Floral Messages from Ottoman Court Embroideries to Anatolian Trousseau Chests*. Translated by Michaela Nierhaus,

Edition Temmen, Bremen.

Thomas, Mary

1953 *Mary Thomas's Embroidery Book*. Hodder & Stoughton, London.

1954 *Mary Thomas's Dictionary of Embroidery Stitches*. Hodder & Stoughton, London.

Wace, A.J.B.

1935 *Mediterranean and Near Eastern Embroideries from the Collection of Mrs. F.H. Cook*. Halton & Company Ltd., London.

Yüksel, Süheylâ Korkusuz

1997 *Nakış: Temel Ders Kitabı*. Milli Eğitim Bakanlığı, İstanbul.

POLITICAL AND ECONOMICAL HISTORY OF THE OTTOMAN EMPIRE

1969 *Keten, Keten Lifi, Keten Tohumu, Keten Yağı, Keten Küspesi*. Türkiye Ticaret Odaları, Sanayi Odaları ve Ticaret Borsaları Birliği, Ankara.

1993 Othmanli, *The Encyclopedia of Islam*, vol. 8, pp. 190–231. E.J. Brill, Leiden.

Atasoy, Nurhan

1992 *Splendors of the Ottoman Sultans*. Wonders, The Memphis International Cultural Series. A Division of City of Memphis, Tennessee and the Directorate General of Monuments and Museums of the Ministry of Culture of the Republic of Turkey, Ankara.

Atıl, Esin

1987 *The Age of Sultan Süleyman, the Magnificent*. Exhibition catalog. National Gallery of Art, Washington and Harry N. Abrams, New York.

Faroqhi, Suraiya

1984 *Towns and Townsmen of Ottoman Anatolia: Trade, Crafts and Food Production in an Urban Setting, 1520–1650*. Cambridge University Press, London.

Fleischer, Cornell H.

1986 *Bureaucrat and Intellectual in the Ottoman Empire: The Historian Mustafa Âli (1541–1600)*. Princeton University Press, Princeton.

İnalcık, Halil

1975 *The Ottoman Empire: The Classical Age 1300–1600*. Translated by Norman Itzkowitz and Colin Imber. Weidenfeld and Nicolson, London.

İnalcık, Halil and Donald Quataert, editors

1996 *An Economic and Social History of the Ottoman Empire, 1300–1914*. Cambridge University Press, Cambridge.

Mansel, Philip

1995 *Constantinople: City of the World's Desire, 1453–1924*. St. Martin's Press, New York.

Quataert, Donald

1993 *Ottoman Manufacturing in the Age of the Industrial Revolution*. Cambridge University Press, Cambridge.

Quataert, Donald, editor

1994 *Manufacturing in the Ottoman Empire and Turkey, 1500–1950*. State University of New York Press, Albany

Shaw, Stanford J.

1977 *Empire of the Gazis: The Rise and Decline of the Ottoman Empire, 1280–1808*. History of the Ottoman Empire and Modern Turkey, vol. 1. Reprint from 1976 edition. Cambridge University Press, Cambridge.

Shaw, Stanford J. and Ezel Kural Shaw

1977 *Reform, Revolution, and Republic: The Rise of Modern Turkey, 1808–1975*. History of the Ottoman Empire and Modern Turkey, vol. 2. Cambridge University Press, Cambridge.

OTTOMAN ART

Brend, Barbara

1991 *Islamic Art*. British Museum Press, London.

Denny, Walter

1981 Turkish Ceramics and Turkish Painting: The Role of Paper Cartoon in Turkish Ceramic Production, *Essays in Islamic Art and Architecture: In Honor of Katharina Otto-Dorn*, pp. 29–35. Edited by Abbas Daneshvari. Undena Publications, Malibu.

Gürsü, Nevber

1988 *The Art of Turkish Weaving: Designs Through the Ages*. Redhouse Press, İstanbul.

Renda, Günsel

1978 Wall Paintings in Turkish Houses, *Fifth International Congress of Turkish Art*, pp. 711–35. Edited by G. Fehér. Akademiai Kiado, Budapest.

Rogers, J.M.

1983 *Islamic Art and Design 1500–1700*. British Museum Publication, London.

Tansuğ, Sabiha

1988 *Türklerde Çiçek Sevgisi ve "Sümbülname."* Ak Yayınları, İstanbul.

Titley, Norah M.

1979 *Plants and Gardens in Persian, Mughal, and Turkish Art*. British Library, London.

TRAVEL WRITINGS AND MEMOIRS

Blunt, Fanny Janet (Sandison), Lady [born 1840]

1918 *My Reminiscences*. John Murray, London.

de Busbecq, Ogier Ghislain [1522–1592]

1968 *The Turkish Letters of Ogier Ghiselin de Busbecq, Imperial Ambassador at Constantinople, 1554–1562*. Translated from the Latin of the Elzevir edition of 1633 by Edward Seymour Forster. Clarendon Press, Oxford.

Craven, Elizabeth, Baroness [1750–1828]

1970 *A Journey Through the Crimea to Constantinople*. Reprint from 1789 Dublin edition. Arno Press, New York.

Della Valle, Pietro [1586–1652]

1990 *The Pilgrim: The Travels of Pietro Della Valle*. Translated, abridged, and introduced by George Bull. Hutchinson, London.

Dodd, Anna Bowman [(Blake)], Mrs. [born 1855]

1903 *In the Palaces of the Sultan*. Mead and Company, New York.

Ferguson, Mary (Nisbet), Mrs. [1777–1855]

1926 *The Letters of Mary Nisbet of Dirleton, Countess of Elgin*. Arranged by Lieut.-Colonel Nisbet Hamilton Grant. John Murray, London.

Garnett, Lucy Mary Jane

1904 *Turkish Life in Town & Country*. George Newnes, London.

1909 *Home Life in Turkey*. The Macmillan Company, New York.

1911 *Turkey of the Ottomans*. Sir I. Pitman & Sons, Ltd., London.

1981 *Balkan Home-Life*. Reprint from 1917 edition. Dodd, Mead & Company, New York.

1982 *The Turkish People: Their Social Life, Religious Beliefs and Institutions and Domestic Life*. Reprint from 1909 edition, Methuen & Co., London. AMS Press, New York.

Haidar, Sherifa Musbah, HRH Princess [born 1908]

1968 *Arabesque*. Revised edition, Sphere, London.

Hornby, Edmund, Mrs. [Emelia Bithynia Maceroni, Lady] [died 1866]

1858 *In and Around Stamboul*. J. Challen & Son, Lindsay & Blakiston, Philadelphia.

Jenkins, Hester Donaldson

1911 *Behind Turkish Lattices: The Story of a Turkish Woman's Life*. Chatto and Windus, London.

Lott, Emmeline
1866 *Harem Life in Egypt and Constantinople; The English Governess in Egypt.* Two volumes, second edition, Richard Bentley, London.

Miller, Barnette
1970 *Beyond the Sublime Porte: the Grand Seraglio of Stambul.* With an introduction by Halide Edib. Reprint from 1931 edition, New Haven. AMS Press, New York.

Morel, Mme
1920 *From an Eastern Embassy.* Lippincott, Philadelphia.

Neave, Dorina Lockhart (Clifton), Lady
1933 *Twenty-Six Years on the Bosphorus.* Grayson & Grayson, London.

Nicolay, Nicolas de [1517–1583]
1989 *Dans l'empire de Soliman le Magnifique/ Nicolas de Nicolay.* Presenté et annoté par Marie-Christine Gomez-Geraud et Stephane Yerasinos. Presses du CNRS, Paris.

Osmanoğlu, Ayşe
1960 *Babam Abdülhamid.* Güven Yayınevi, İstanbul.

Paine, Caroline
1859 *Tent and Harem: Notes of an Oriental Trip.* D. Appleton and Company, New York.

Pardoe, Julia [1806–1862]
1837 *The City of the Sultan.* Two volumes. H. Colburn, London.
1855? *The Beauties of the Bosphorus.* Virtue and Co., London.

Penzer, N.M. (Norman Mosley) [born 1892]
1975 *The Harem: An Account of the Institution as it Existed in the Palace of the Turkish Sultans with a History of the Grand Seraglio from its Foundation to the Present Time.* Reprint from 1937 edition, J.B. Lippincott, Philadelphia. AMS Press, New York.

Pick, Christopher, editor and compiler
1988 *Embassy to Constantinople: The Travels of Lady Mary Wortley Montagu.* New Amsterdam Books, New York.

Porter, David
1835 *Constantinople and its Environs: A Series of Letters, Exhibiting the Actual State of the Manners, Customs, and Habits of the Turks, Jews, and Greeks, as Modified by the Policy of Sultan Mahmoud by an American Long Resident at Constantinople.* Two volumes. Harper & Brothers, New York.

Saz, Leyla [1850–1936]
1994 *The Imperial Harem of the Sultans: Daily Life at The Ciragan Palace During the 19th Century: Memoirs of Leyla (Saz) Hanimefendi.* Translated from the French by Landon Thomas. Peva Publications, Beyoglu, İstanbul.

Tugay, Emine Foat [born 1897]
1963 *Three Centuries: Family Chronicles of Turkey and Egypt.* With a Foreword by the Dowager Marchioness of Reading. Oxford University Press, London, New York and Toronto.

Ünüvar, Safiye
1964 *Saray Hatıralarım.* Cağaloğlu Yayınevi, İstanbul

Whaley, Thomas [1766–1800]
1906 *Buck Whaley's Memoirs: Including his Journey to Jerusalem, written by himself in 1797 and now first published from the recently recovered manuscript.* Edited, with Introduction and notes by Sir Edward Sullivan, Bart. Alexander Moring, Ltd., London.

White, Charles [1793–1861]
1845 *Three Years in Constantinople or Domestic Manners of the Turks in 1844.* Henry Colburn, London.

Zeyneb, Hanum
1913 *A Turkish Woman's European Impressions.* Edited by Grace Ellison. J.B. Lippincott Company, Philadelphia and London.

OTTOMAN SOCIAL LIFE

And, Metin
1994 *Istanbul in the 16th Century: The City, the Palace, Daily Life.* Akbank, İstanbul.

Dengler, Ian C.
1978 Turkish Women in the Ottoman Empire: The Classical Age, *Women in the Muslim World*, pp. 229–44. Edited by Lois Beck and Nikki Keddie. Harvard University Press, Cambridge.

Gerber, Haim
1980 Social and Economic Position of Women in an Ottoman City, Bursa 1600–1700, *International Journal of Middle East Studies (IJMES)*, vol. 12, no. 1, pp. 231–44. Cambridge University Press, Cambridge.
1988 *Economy and Society in an Ottoman City, Bursa 1600–1700.* Institute of Asian and African Studies, The Hebrew University, Jerusalem.

Goodwin, Godfrey
1997 *The Private World of Ottoman Women.* Saqi Books, London.

Göçek, Fatma Müge and Marc David Baer
1997 Social Boundaries of Ottoman Women's Experience in Eighteenth-Century Galata Court Records, *Women in the Ottoman Empire: Middle Eastern Women in the Early Modern Era*, pp. 48–65. Edited by Madeline Zilfi. E.J. Brill, Leiden, New York, and Köln.

Graham-Brown, Sarah
1988 *Images of Women: The Portrayal of Women in Photography of the Middle East 1860–1950.* Columbia University Press, New York.

Kayaoğlu, I. Gündağ
1998 *Eski İstanbul'da Gündelik Hayat.* Aksoy Yayıncılık, Istanbul.

Lewis, Bernard
1963 *Istanbul and the Civilization of the Ottoman Empire.* The University of Oklahoma Press, Norman.

Lewis, Raphaela.
1971 *Everyday Life in Ottoman Turkey.* G.P. Putnam's Sons, New York, and B.T. Batsford Ltd., London.

Micklewright, Nancy
1989 Late-Nineteeth-Century Ottoman Wedding Costumes as Indicators of Social Change. *Muqarnas*, vol. 6, pp. 162–73. Edited by Oleg Gabar. E.J. Brill, Leiden.
1990 Looking at the Past: Nineteenth-Century Images of Constantinople as Historical Documents, *Expedition*, vol. 32, no. 1, pp. 24–33.
MS Women's Dress in Nineteenth-Century Istanbul: Mirror of a Changing Society. PhD dissertation, History of Art, University of Pennsylvania, 1986.

Pierce, Leslie P.
1993 *The Imperial Harem: Women and Sovereignty in the Ottoman Empire.* Oxford University Press, Oxford.
1997 Seniority, Sexuality, and Social Order: The Vocabulary of Gender in Early Modern Ottoman Society, *Women in the Ottoman Empire: Middle Eastern Women in the Early Modern Era*, pp. 169–96. Edited by Madeline Zilfi. E.J. Brill, Leiden, New York, and Köln.

Scarce, Jennifer
1987 *Women's Costume of the Near and Middle East.* Unwin Hyman, London.
1988 Principles of Ottoman Turkish Costume, *Costume*, no. 22, pp. 8–31. The Costume Society, London.
1996 *Domestic Culture in the Middle East: An Exploration of the Household Interior.* National Museum of Scotland, Edinburgh.

Index